The Quotable Billionaire

Also by Steven D. Price

TEACHING RIDING AT SUMMER CAMP (The Stephen Greene Press, 1972)

PANORAMA OF AMERICAN HORSES (Westover/Crown, 1973)

CIVIL RIGHTS, Vols. 1 & 2 (Facts On File, 1973)

GET A HORSE!: BASICS OF BACKYARD HORSEKEEPING (Viking, 1974)

TAKE ME HOME: THE RISE OF COUNTRY-AND-WESTERN MUSIC (Praeger, 1974)

THE SECOND-TIME SINGLE MAN'S SURVIVAL HANDBOOK,
with William J. Gordon (Praeger, 1975)

OLD AS THE HILLS: THE STORY OF BLUEGRASS MUSIC (Viking, 1975)

HORSEBACK VACATION GUIDE (The Stephen Greene Press, 1975)

SCHOOLING TO SHOW: BASICS OF HUNTER-JUMPER TRAINING, with Anthony D'Ambrosio, Jr. (Viking, 1978)

THE WHOLE HORSE CATALOG, Editorial Director
(Simon & Schuster, 1979, revised 1985, 1993, 1998)

THE COMPLETE BOOK OF HORSE & SADDLE EQUIPMENT
with Elwyn Hartley Edwards, (Quarto/Exeter, 1981)

RIDING'S A JOY, with Joy Slater (Doubleday, 1982)

ALL THE KING'S HORSES: THE STORY OF THE BUDWEISER CLYDESDALES
(Viking, 1983)

The Beautiful Baby Naming Book (Simon & Schuster, 1984)

Riding For A Fall (Tor Books, 1988)

The Polo Primer, with Charles Kauffman (The Stephen Greene Press, 1989)

The Ultimate Fishing Guide (HarperCollins, 1996)

Caught Me A Big 'Un, with Jimmy Houston (Pocket Books, 1996)

The Complete Book of the American Quarter Horse (The Lyons Press, 1998)

Two Bits' Book of the American Quarter Horse (The Lyons Press, 1999)

The Quotable Horse Lover (The Lyons Press, 1999)

Essential Riding (The Lyons Press, 2000)

The Illustrated Horseman's Dictionary (The Lyons Press, 2000)

The Greatest Horse Stories Ever Told (The Lyons Press, 2001)

Classic Horse Stories (The Lyons Press, 2002)

1001 Smartest Things Ever Said (The Lyons Press, 2004)

1001 Dumbest Things Ever Said (The Lyons Press, 2004)

1001 Insults, Put-Downs And Comebacks (The Lyons Press, 2005)

1001 Funniest Things Ever Said (The Lyons Press, 2006)

THE BEST ADVICE EVER GIVEN (The Lyons Press, 2006)

1001 BEST THINGS EVER SAID ABOUT HORSES (The Lyons Press, 2006)

1001 BEST THINGS EVER SAID ABOUT CALIFORNIA
(The Lyons Press, 2007)

THE HORSEMAN'S DICTIONARY, Revised Edition, with Jessie Shiers,
(The Lyons Press, 2007)

The Quotable Billionaire

Advice And Reflections From and For the Real, Former, Almost, and Wanna-Be Super-Rich . . . and Others

Edited and with an Introduction by
Steven D. Price

Skyhorse Publishing

Skyhorse Publishing books may be purchased in bulk at special discounts for sales promotion, corporate gifts, fund-raising, or educational purposes. Special editions can also be created to specifications. For details, contact the Special Sales Department, Skyhorse Publishing, 555 Eighth Avenue, Suite 903, New York, NY 10018 or info@skyhorsepublishing.com.

www.skyhorsepublishing.com

10 9 8 7 6 5 4 3 2 1

Library of Congress Cataloging-in-Publication Data

The quotable billionaire: advice and reflections from and for the real, former, almost, and wanna-be super-rich and others / edited and with an Introduction by Steven D. Price.
p. cm.
Includes bibliographical references and index.
ISBN 978-1-60239-729-3 (alk. paper)
1. Wealth. 2. Success. 3. Leadership. I. Price, Steven D.
HB251.Q86 2009
658.4'09–dc22
2009015794

Printed in the United States of America

Money is like a sixth sense without which you cannot make a complete use of the other five.

—W. Somerset Maugham

1,000,000,000
FEDERAL RESERVE NOTE
FF 95594731 A
F6
THE UNITED STATES OF AMERICA
1,000,000,000
THIS NOTE IS LEGAL TENDER FOR ALL DEBTS, PUBLIC AND PRIVATE
SERIES 2003 A
1,000,000,000
FEDERAL RESERVE NOTE
FF 95594731 A
F6
THE UNITED STATES OF AMERICA
1,000,000,000
FF 95594731 A
THIS NOTE IS LEGAL TENDER FOR ALL DEBTS, PUBLIC AND PRIVATE
SERIES 2003 A
ONE BILLION DOLLARS
1,000,000,000
F6
THE UNITED STATES OF AMERICA
1,000,000,000
FF 95594731 A
THIS NOTE IS LEGAL TENDER FOR ALL DEBTS, PUBLIC AND PRIVATE
SERIES 2003 A
ONE BILLION DOLLARS

Contents

1,000,000,000
THE UNITED STATES OF AMERICA
1,000,000,000
FEDERAL RESERVE NOTE
FF 95594731 A
F6
1,000,000,000
FF 95594731 A
THIS NOTE IS LEGAL TENDER FOR ALL DEBTS, PUBLIC AND PRIVATE
SERIES 2003 A
ONE BILLION DOLLARS
1,000,000,000
THE UNITED STATES OF AMERICA
1,000,000,000
FF 95594731 A
THIS NOTE IS LEGAL TENDER FOR ALL DEBTS, PUBLIC AND PRIVATE
SERIES 2003 A
1,000,000,000
THE UNITED STATES OF AMERICA
1,000,000,000
FEDERAL RESERVE NOTE
FF 95594731 A
F6
1,000,000,000
FF 95594731 A
THIS NOTE IS LEGAL TENDER FOR ALL DEBTS, PUBLIC AND PRIVATE
SERIES 2003 A
ONE BILLION DOLLARS

Introduction

It wasn't too long ago that millionaires were such rarities that they were held in awe. When John D.'s descendants objected to a line in a coffee commercial of the 1980s that "a better coffee Rockefeller's money can't buy" and the line was changed to "a better coffee a millionaire's money can't buy," the impact of the message wasn't diminished in the least. There was a handful of millionaires, and then there were the rest of us.

The wealth explosion during the 1990s and the first decade of this century changed all that. Executives at the top of their corporate and law-firm ladders received compensation packages of salaries, stock options, "golden parachutes," and other benefits that pushed their worth over the million-dollar mark; as their compensation rose, so did that of middle-management and legal associations to the point that their amassing a million dollars over a few years was not out of reach. Professional baseball, football, and basketball players as well as other athletes were offered astronomical contracts as a matter of course. A million-dollar lottery payout became hardly worth mentioning on television newscasts. And then came the stock market's "dot-com bubble" era in which even modest investors saw their net worth increase manyfold. Millionaires became not quite a dime a dozen, but certainly not the rare species they had once been.

When envying millionaires became old hat, the world needed another category to drool over. Enter: the billionaire. Not that billionaires hadn't existed, but there were very few. According to *Forbes* magazine, which started keeping tabs on the mega-rich the way the *Baseball Encyclopedia* provides statistics for the national pastime, in 1982 there were 13 billionaires. The number increased to 15 a year later, but dropped down to 12 in 1984. Then came the deluge. Nineteen eighty-six saw 13 billionaires in the world, 26 in 1986, and 49 in 1987. By 1989, the number had risen precipitously to 82, and by 1990, the *Forbes* survey reported a total of 99. The number kept rising, thanks to entrepreneurism, investment opportunities, and the Reagan administration's tax legislation that allowed the super-rich to keep their money until in 2008 there were 1,125 billionaires worldwide. And by "worldwide," four of the top ten in net worth live in India, two in the U.S., and one each in Mexico, Sweden, Russia, and Germany (see the index for a list of the top 25 on the *Forbes* list).

This year's *Forbes* list numbers only—*only*? you might respond—793. This 30 percent decline reflects what everyone knows—and has experienced: The world's economy has tanked. Still, there's no reason to run a bazaar for the majority of people who slipped off the list; at a net worth now of "only" hundreds of millions of dollars, they're not exactly agonizing over where their next Rolls-Royce or six-pack of Beluga caviar is coming from.

The views of the mega-rich on money and its acquisition, benefits, and pitfalls—should be instructive. A problem, however, is that most of the mega-rich have chosen not to express their views or, if they did, said nothing of lasting value. That's not their fault: Nowhere is it written that anyone must be articulate about money, even people with plenty of it.

But those billionaires who have spoken have made, by and large, entertaining and instructive comments and reflections. So have former billionaires, almost billionaires, close-to-being billionaires, and would-have-been-billionaires-if-they-had-lived-now ("honorary" billionaires, such as Thomas Edison and George Eastman fall into this last group). And, because others who don't fit into any of the above categories have said equally insightful, provocative, and even entertaining things on the subject of wealth, they're included too.

You'll find those billionaires whom you'd expect to find, such as Bill Gates ("Be nice to nerds. Chances are you'll end up working for one."); Oprah Winfrey ("I don't think of myself as a poor, deprived ghetto girl who made good. I think of myself as somebody who from an early age knew I was responsible for myself, and I had to make good."); Warren Buffett ("Of the billionaires I have known, money just brings out the basic traits in them. If they were jerks before they had money, they are simply jerks with a billion dollars."); and Sam Walton ("Capital isn't scarce; vision is.").

There are also billionaires who might not spring to mind, like fashion designer Giorgio Armani ("I supposed it would have been great to invent something as classic and enduring as the tuxedo. But if I was collecting royalties, I wish I'd invented the corkscrew."); Steven Spielberg ("Why pay a dollar for a bookmark? Why not use the dollar for a bookmark?"); and Queen Eizabth II ("It's all to do with the training: you can do a lot if you're properly trained.").

And then there are others whose reflections on the money were worth including: Society interior decorator Billy Baldwin ("Rich Palm Beach clients all wanted the same kind of different thing."); cowboy humorist Will Rogers ("Don't gamble; take all your savings and buy some good stock and hold it till it goes up, then sell it. If it don't go up, don't buy it."); and mobster John Gotti ("I would be a billionaire if I was looking to be a selfish boss.").

With the world economy heading south, at least at this writing, one might wonder why assembling a book of quotations by and about very wealthy people makes sense. For one thing, their views on money, its acquisition, benefits and pitfalls, and indeed the world in general can prove instructive to those of us who hope to increase our own net worth, especially in the teeth of this economic tsunami.

Another reason is escapism. The Great Depression caused people to find a few hours' respite from their troubles by going to movies, listening to the radio, and reading books. We're doing much of the same thing during these hard times with the addition of television, video games, and cellular technology. In that spirit, dipping into this book might prove diverting. I hope so—we could certainly use it.

Special thanks to Kathleen Go, who as an editor is one in a billion.

Steven D. Price

New York, New York
April 1, 2009

1

Wealth: In the Abstract and in the Concrete

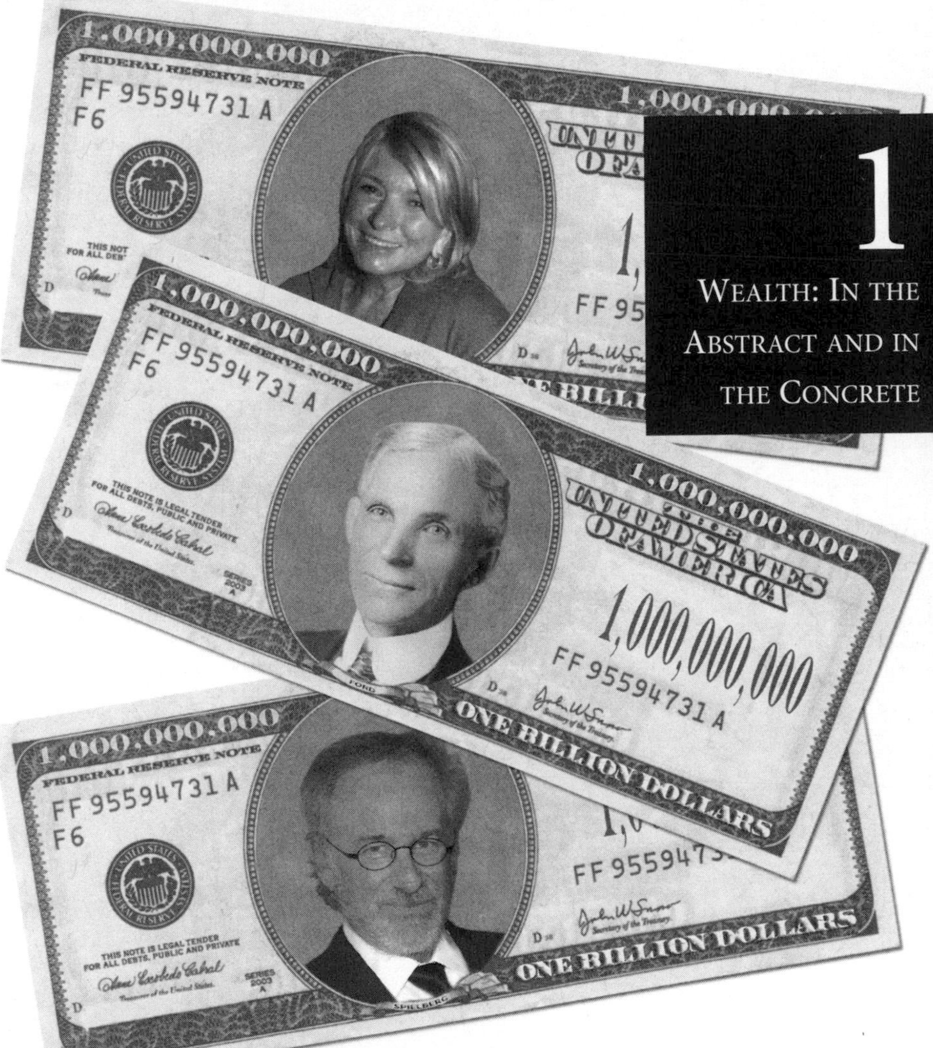

Anyone can be a millionaire, but to become a billionaire you need an astrologer.

—J. P. Morgan

I believe that the power to make money is a gift from God.

—John D. Rockefeller

I'm not a paranoid deranged millionaire. Goddammit, I'm a billionaire.

—Howard Hughes

If you can actually count your money, then you are not really a rich man.

—J. Paul Getty

There's a certain part of the contented majority who love anybody who is worth a billion dollars.

—John Kenneth Galbraith, regarding political candidate H. Ross Perot

Loco Dempsey: You don't think he's a little old?
Schatze Page: Wealthy men are never old.

—from the film *How to Marry a Millionaire*

It isn't necessary to be rich and famous to be happy.
It's only necessary to be rich.

—Alan Alda

In suggesting gifts, money is appropriate, and one size fits all.

—William Handolph Hearst

Fortune has something of the nature of a woman.
If she is too intensely wooed,
she commonly goes the further away.

—Charles V

A feast is made for laughter, and wine makes life merry, but
money is the answer for everything.

—Ecclesiastes 10:19

This, then, is held to be the duty of the man of Wealth: First, to set an example of modest, unostentatious living, shunning display or extravagance; to provide moderately for the legitimate wants of those dependent upon him; and after doing so to consider all surplus revenues which come to him simply as trust funds, which he is called upon to administer, and strictly bound as a matter of duty to administer in the manner which, in his judgment, is best calculated to produce the most beneficial results for the community.

—Andrew Carnegie, *The Gospel of Wealth*

The rich are not born sceptical or cynical.
They are made that way by events, circumstances.

—J. Paul Getty

Look at all the billionaires. If I know 15 billionaires,
I know 13 unhappy people.

—Russell Simmons

Some people on the [*Forbes*] list are in their thirties and are worth at least $10 billion. But it's good to be on the list.

—Ronald Lauder

I have been insane on the subject of moneymaking all my life.

—Cornelius Vanderbilt

Of the billionaires I have known, money just brings out the basic traits in them. If they were jerks before they had money, they are simply jerks with a billion dollars.

—Warren Buffett

I know of nothing more despicable and pathetic than a man who devotes all the hours of the waking day to the making of money for money's sake.

—John D. Rockefeller

If you've literally been worrying, "Will the money last until the end of the week?" you will never, ever complain about having money.

—J. K. Rowling

All money means to me is a pride in accomplishment.

—Ray Kroc

There is no class so pitiably wretched as that which possesses money and nothing else.

—Andrew Carnegie

Money is like water. Block its flow and it will stagnate.

—Mohammad bin Rashid Al Maktoum

Becoming wealthy is like playing Monopoly . . . the person who can accumulate the most assets wins the game.

—Noel Whittaker

Money is plentiful for those who understand the simple laws which govern its acquisition.

—George Clason

Money, which represents the prose of life, and which is hardly spoken of in parlors without an apology, is, in its effects and laws, as beautiful as roses.

—Ralph Waldo Emerson

I have a million dollars in the stock market, because if I lose a million dollars, I don't personally care.

—Suze Orman

Annual income twenty pounds, annual expenditure nineteen six, result happiness. Annual income twenty pounds, annual expenditure twenty pound ought and six, result misery.

—the character Mr. Mikawber, in Charles Dickens's *David Copperfield*

Dollars have never been known to produce character, and character will never be produced by money.

—W. K. Kellogg

Money is just a way of keeping score.

—H. L. Hunt

A billion dollars isn't what it used to be.

—Nelson Bunker Hunt

No matter how rich you become, how famous or powerful, when you die the size of your funeral will still pretty much depend on the weather.

—Michael Pritchard

Pola Debevoise: I want to marry Rockefeller.
Schatze Page: Which one?
Pola Debevoise: I don't care.

—from the film *How to Marry a Millionaire*

I have enjoyed the personal use of money, but I have gotten the greatest satisfaction from using it to advance my beliefs in human relations, human values.

—Winthrop Rockefeller

Life is a game. Money is how we keep score.

—Ted Turner

I made 50 million bucks yesterday.
That's a flameout I could get used to.

—Conrad Black

Permit me to issue and control the money of a nation,
and I care not who makes its laws.

—Mayer Amschel Rothschild

I liked money more than going to school.

—Norton Simon

Money is God in action.

—Frederick "Reverend Ike" Eikerenkootter

When a man says money can do anything,
that settles it: he hasn't got any.

—George Bernard Shaw

Millions not always helps achive [*sic*] what we wants from life.

—Aristotle Onassis

If you want to know what God thinks of money,
just look at the people he gave it to.

—Dorothy Parker

The man who has won millions at the cost of his conscience is a failure.

—Bertie Charles Forbes

Make money, money by fair means if you can, if not,
but any means money.

—Horace

No one can earn a million dollars honestly.

—William Jennings Bryan

You can't tell a millionaire's son from a billionaire's.

—Vance Packard, on democracy at prep schools, from his best-selling book *The Status Seekers*

A billion here and a billion there, and pretty soon you're talking real money.

—Senator Everett Dirkson

Nothing is more admirable than the fortitude with which millionaires tolerate the disadvantages of their wealth.

—Rex Stout

My religion? Well, my dear, I am a Millionaire. That is my religion.

—George Bernard Shaw, *Major Barbara*

Is the rich world aware of how four billion of the six billion live? If we were aware, we would want to help out, we'd want to get involved.

—Bill Gates

People who grow rich almost always improve their sex life. More people want to have sex with them. That's just the way human beings work. Money is power. Power is an aphrodisiac. Money did not make me happy. But it definitely improved my sex life.

—Felix Dennis

One dollar for eternal happiness? I'd be happier with the dollar.

—Charles Montgomery "Monty" Burns

If one is rich and one's a woman, one can be quite misunderstood.

—Katharine Graham

Greed is all right, by the way . . . I think greed is healthy. You can be greedy and still feel good about yourself.

—Ivan Boesky

Any man who does not carry freedom in his wallet has no value to his life, or the flexibility to switch between cash or points.

—J. P. Morgan

Money: power at its most liquid.

—Mason Cooley

I no longer want to be rich because I am rich.

—Uri Geller

Money "talks" because money is a metaphor, a transfer, and a bridge. Like words and language, money is a storehouse of communally achieved work, skill, and experience. . . . It gives great spatial expansion and control to political organizations, just as writing does, or the calendar.

—Marshall McLuhan

After a certain point, money is meaningless.
It ceases to be the goal. The game is what counts.

—Aristotle Onassis

I know of nothing more despicable and pathetic than a man who devotes all the hours of the waking day to the making of money for money's sake.

—John D. Rockefeller

Though I am grateful for the blessings of wealth, it hasn't changed who I am. My feet are still on the ground. I'm just wearing better shoes.

—Oprah Winfrey

The only way not to think about money is to have a great deal of it.

—Edith Wharton

The only question with wealth is,
what do you do with it?

—John D. Rockefeller

I wish I wasn't . . . There's nothing good that comes out of that. You get more visibility as a result of it.

—Bill Gates, on being the world's richest man

As I started getting rich, I started thinking, "What the hell am I going to do with all this money?" . . . You have to learn to give.

—Ted Turner

The happiest time in a man's life is when he is in the red hot pursuit of a dollar with a reasonable prospect of overtaking it.

—Josh Billings

Money is like manure. You have to spread it around or it smells.

—J. Paul Getty

[similarly:] Money is like muck, not good except it be spread.

—Sir Francis Bacon

It's easier to get rich than it is to explain not getting rich.

—E. James Rohn

The rich get richer. Not only because they have surpluses with which to invest, but because of the overriding emotional release they experience from having wealth.

—Stuart Wilde

I didn't want to be greedy. It's a mark of bad character and I always believed that pigs go the slaughterhouse.

—Walter Annenberg

When you earn money and spend money every day, anybody can know the difference between a million and three. But when you vote money away there really is not any difference between a million and three.

—Gertrude Stein

I have a problem with too much money. I can't reinvest it fast enough, and because I reinvest it, more money comes in. Yes, the rich do get richer.

—Robert Kiyosaki

What good is money if it can't inspire terror in your fellow man?

—Charles Montgomery "Monty" Burns

Money often costs too much.

—Ralph Waldo Emerson

People who know how much they're worth aren't usually worth that much.

—Nelson Bunker Hunt

If you would know the value of money, go and try to borrow some.

—Benjamin Franklin

I'm going to miss Blockbuster. I'm gonna miss being CEO and all that stuff. We had an atmosphere where everybody was happy. When people make money, they're happy.

—Wayne Huizenga

If you have to ask how much it costs, you can't afford it.

—J. P. Morgan, when asked how much a yacht costs

Anything that has to do with money, I want to be in that business.

—Robert Johnson

If money is your hope for independence, you will never have it. The only real security that a man will have in this world is a reserve of knowledge, experience, and ability.

—Henry Ford

Money is good for bribing yourself through the inconveniences of life.

—Gottfried Reinhardt

Money gives me more energy than all the granola bars in the world.

—Mason Cooley

Anybody who thinks money will make you happy hasn't got money.

—David Geffen

I don't want to become too rich because not one rich person controls richness, but is controlled by it.

—A. P. Giannini

Wealth is power. With wealth many things are possible.

—George Clason

The real measure of your wealth is how much you'd be worth if you lost all your money.

—source unknown

Without money, honor is merely a disease.

—Jean Racine

Money, like vodka, turns a person into an eccentric.

—Anton Chekhov

Money doesn't mind if we say it's evil, it goes from strength to strength. It's a fiction, an addiction, and a tacit conspiracy.

—Martin Amis

My foundations support people in the country who care about an open society. It's their work that I'm supporting. So it's not me doing it. But I can empower them. I can support them, and I can help them.

—George Soros

I have enough money to satisfy myself for a lifetime.

—Stevie Wonder

I'd like to live like a poor man with lots of money.

—Pablo Picasso

If you make money your god, it will plague you like the devil.

—Henry Fielding

If there was no money in poetry,
there was certainly no poetry in money, and so it was all even.

—Robert Graves

Money is truthful. If a man speaks of his honor, make him pay cash.

—Robert A. Heinlein

Becoming wealthy is not a matter of how much you earn, who your parents are, or what you do . . . it is a matter of managing your money properly.

—Noel Whittaker

The rule is not to talk about money with people who have much more or much less than you.

—Katherine Whitehorn

Money is like a sixth sense without which you cannot make a complete use of the other five.

—W. Somerset Maugham

Money is a poor man's credit card.

—Marshall McLuhan

There is no class so pitiably wretched as that which possesses money and nothing else.

—Andrew Carnegie

I'd say it's been my biggest problem all my life . . . it's money. It takes a lot of money to make these dreams come true.

—Walt Disney

When it's a question of money, everybody is of the same religion.

—Voltaire

The secret point of money and power in America is neither the things that money can buy nor power for power's sake . . . but absolute personal freedom, mobility, privacy.

—Joan Didion

Rich people always have a certain degree of debt. Apparently it helps to reduce taxes. I'm not so hot on the bean-counting side.

—Felix Dennis

Money won is twice as sweet as money earned.

—"Fast Eddie" Felson in *The Color Of Money*

Money will never make you happy and happy will never make you money. That may be a wise crack, but I doubt it.

—Groucho Marx in *The Cocoanuts*

Money cannot buy peace of mind. It cannot heal ruptured relationships, or build meaning into a life that has none.

—Richard M. DeVos

Money is better than poverty, if only for financial reasons.

—Woody Allen

All money nowadays seems to be produced
with a natural homing instinct for the Treasury.

—Prince Philip, Duke of Edinburgh

Money's a horrid thing to follow, but a charming thing to meet.

—Henry James, *Portrait of a lady*

Money can move the gods.

—Chinese proverb

There's no reason to be the richest man in the cemetery.
You can't do any business from there.

—Colonel Harland Sanders

I resolved to stop accumulating and begin the infinitely more serious and difficult task of wise distribution.

—Andrew Carnegie

I was never interested in money. I always looked down on it. But now that I have less money, I see that without money, you cannot do much. Everything in the end is about money.

—Farah Pahlavi

A rich man is nothing but a poor man with money.

—W. C. Fields

It is more difficult for a rich man to enter the kingdom of God than it is for a camel to pass through the eye of a needle.

—The New Testament, Mark 10:25

Money can't buy me love.

—The Beatles

The rich aren't like us—they pay less taxes.

—Peter de Vries

The rich are the scum of the earth in every country.

—G. K. Chesterton

The richest man is the one who feels rich enough.

—Leonid S. Sukhorukov

Money gives me pleasure all the time.

—Hillaire Belloc

To turn $100 into $110 is work.
To turn $100 million into $110 million is inevitable.

—Edgar Bronfman, Sr.

A little more moderation would be good. Of course, my life hasn't exactly been one of moderation.

—Donald Trump

Sir, money, money, the most charming of all things; money, which will say more in one moment than the most elegant lover can in years. Perhaps you will say a man is not young; I answer he is rich. He is not genteel, handsome, witty, brave, good-humoured, but he is rich, rich, rich, rich, rich—that one word contradicts everything you can say against him.

—Henry Fielding, *The Miser*

Wealth and poverty are different worlds on the same planet.

—Leonid S. Sukhorukov

Financial education needs to become a part of our national curriculum and scoring systems so that it's not just the rich kids that learn about money . . . it's all of us.

—David Bach

Money indeed may be considered as the most universal and expressive of all languages.

—Samuel Butler

Take dead aim on the rich boys. Get them in the crosshairs and take them down.

—Herman Blume

Money doesn't talk, it swears.

—Bob Dylan

A business that makes nothing but money is a poor kind of business.

—Henry Ford

I make too much money to be a front man.

—Robert Johnson

There are people who have money and people who are rich.

—Coco Chanel

Money is a terrible master but an excellent servant.

—P. T. Barnum

Money is a singular thing. It ranks with love as man's greatest source of joy. And with death as his greatest source of anxiety.

—John Kenneth Galbraith

If you're given a choice between money and sex appeal, take the money. As you get older, the money will become your sex appeal.

—Katharine Hepburn

While few judges or prosecutors would be afraid to exercise their perfectly legitimate discretion in favour of an ordinary man, not to mention a minority group member, most would be terrified to exercise the same discretion for someone politically, financially, or socially powerful.

—Conrad Black

Children need money. As they grow older they need more money. They need money for essentially the same reasons that adults need money. They need to buy stuff. . . . They need it regardless of whether they get good grades, violate a family rule, or offend a parent.

—Donald C. Medeiros

Always be the only person who can sign your checks.

—Oprah Winfrey

This, then, is held to be the duty of the man of wealth: First, to set an example of modest, unostentatious living, shunning display or extravagance; to provide moderately for the legitimate wants of those dependent upon him; and, after doing so, to consider all surplus revenues which come to him simply as trust funds, which he is called upon to administer, and strictly bound as a matter of duty to administer in the manner which, in his judgment, is best calculated to produce the most beneficial results for the community—the man of wealth thus becoming the mere trustee and agent for his poorer brethren, bringing to their service his superior wisdom, experience and ability to administer, doing for them better than they would or could do for themselves.

—Andrew Carnegie

Greed is all right, by the way . . . I think greed is healthy. You can be greedy and still feel good about yourself.

—Ivan Boesky

The public be damned.

—William Henry Vanderbilt, when asked whether the public should be consulted about a change in a train schedule

I intend to be the greatest golfer in the world, the finest film producer in Hollywood, the greatest pilot in the world, and the richest man in the world.

—Howard Hughes

The biggest mistake that I see people of wealth making is having a single-minded focus on investment returns with no thought about their spending patterns. At the end of the day, expense control plays a larger role in the success of a financial program than the entire array of specific investments.

—A. Michael Lipper

Money was never a big motivation for me, except as a way to keep score. The real excitement is playing the game.

—Donald Trump

I'm not really interested in making money. That always come as the result of success, but it's not been my goal, and I've had a tough time proving that to people.

—Steven Spielberg

Money itch is a bad thing. I never had that trouble.

—A. P. Giannini

The more I study the wealthy in an effort to learn how to help more people around the world become one of them, I'm stunned by how many people are actually not rich.

—David Bach

The rich swell up with pride, the poor from hunger.

—Sholom Aleichem

The amount of money you have has got nothing to do with what you earn. People earning a million dollars a year can have no money and . . . People earning $35,000 a year can be quite well off. It's not what you earn, it's what you spend.

—Paul Clitheroe

Owning a home is a keystone of wealth . . .
both financial affluence and emotional security.

—Suze Orman

God gave me my money. I believe the power to make money is a gift from God . . . to be developed and used to the best of our ability for the good of mankind. Having been endowed with the gift I possess, I believe it is my duty to make money and still more money and to use the money I make for the good of my fellow man according to the dictates of my conscience.

—John D. Rockefeller

As a vast social metaphor, bridge, or translator, money—like writing—speeds up exchange and tightens the bonds of interdependence in any community.

—Marshall McLuhan

To fulfill a dream, to be allowed to sweat over lonely labor, to be given a chance to create, is the meat and potatoes of life. The money is the gravy.

—Bette Davis

Money is the last enemy that shall never be subdued. While there is flesh there is money—or the want of money, but money is always on the brain so long as there is a brain in reasonable order.

—Samuel Butler

There is no amount of money in the world that will make you comfortable if you are not comfortable with yourself.

—Stuart Wilde

Here, take the money, Ben. It's not like people.
It's got no memory. It don't think.

—from the film *Body and Soul*

Most of the money given by rich people in "charity" is made up of conscience money, "ransom," political bribery, and bids for titles.

—George Bernard Shaw, *Socialism for Millionaires*

The civility which money will purchase,
is rarely extended to those who have none.

—Charles Dickens

A fool and his money are lucky enough to get together in the first place.

—from the film *Wall Street*

The love of money is the root of all evil.

—The New Testament, 1 Timothy 6:10

The want of money is the root of all evil.

—Samuel Butler

[also:] The *lack* of money is the root of all evil.

—Frederick "Reverend Ike" Eikerenkootter

Liking money like I like it, is nothing less than mysticism. Money is a glory.

—Salvador Dali

I don't care half so much about making money as
I do about making my point, and coming out ahead.

—Cornelius "Commodore" Vanderbilt

Money alone sets all the world in motion.

—Publius Syrus

Get money; still get money, boy,
no matter by what means.

—Ben Jonson, *Every Man in his Humour*

Remember that time is money.

—Benjamin Franklin, *Advice to a Young Tradesman*

He that wants money, means, and content is
without three good friends.

—William Shakespeare, *As You Like It*

Put not your trust in money, but put your money in trust.

—Oliver Wendell Holmes, *The Autocrat of the Breakfast-Table*

Nothing comes amiss; so money comes withal.

—William Shakespeare, *The Taming of the Shrew*

If money go before, all ways do lie open.

—William Shakespeare, *The Merry Wives of Windsor*

After you marry, every asset either of you acquires is jointly held. That's why you both need to be in sync on your long-term financial goals, from paying off the mortgage to putting away for retirement. Ideally, you should talk about all this before you wed. If you don't, you can end up deeply frustrated and financially spent.

—Suze Orman

How pleasant it is to have money!

—Arthur Hugh Clough

I've never lived in a building without my name on it.

—Ivanka Trump

[The rich] are indeed rather possessed by their money than possessors.

—Richard Burton, *The Anatomy of Melancholy*

I get angry when someone calls me only rich . . .
I am happy with my social personality and my generosity.

—Sakip Sabanci

. . . the consoling proximity of millionaires . . .

—F. Scott Fitzgerald, *The Great Gatsby*

It is generally agreed that few men are made better by affluence or exaltation.

—Samuel Johnson

Let us all be happy and live within our means,
even if we have to borrow the money to do it with.

—Artemus Ward

Some people find an interest in making money, and though they appear to be slaving, many actually enjoy every minute of their work.

—Walter Annenberg

A man who has a million dollars is as well off as if he were rich.

—John Jacob Astor

The only thing I like about rich people is their money.

—Nancy Astor

Those who spend too fast never grow rich.

—Honoré de Balzac

A rich man told me recently that a liberal is a man who tells other people what to do with their money.

—Amiri Baraka

Stand not too near the rich man lest he destroy thee—
and not too far away lest he forget thee.

—Aneurin Bevan

It's easy to have principles when you're rich.
The important thing is to have principles when you're poor.

—Ray Kroc

When I wake up in the morning,
I feel like a billionaire without paying taxes.

—Ernie Banks

Biggest problem? Well, I'd say it's been my biggest problem all my life. MONEY. It takes a lot of money to make these dreams come true. From the very start it was a problem. Getting the money to open Disneyland. About seventeen million it took. And we had everything mortgaged including my personal insurance.

—Walt Disney

I'm a millionaire, I'm a multi-millionaire.
I'm filthy rich. You know why I'm a multi-millionaire?
'Cause multi-millions like what I do.

—Michael Moore

A rich man is nothing but a poor man with money.

—W. C. Fields

One of the reasons the rich get richer, the poor get poorer, and the middle class struggles in debt is because the subject of money is taught at home, not at school.

—Robert Kiyosaki

Some people think they are worth a lot of money just because they have it.

—Fannie Hurst

I would be a billionaire if I was looking to be a selfish boss. That's not me.

—John Gotti

It doesn't matter who you vote for.
It's still the same billionaires that run the world.

—Geezer Butler

Making money is a hobby that will complement
any other hobbies you have, beautifully.

—Scott Alexander

Money is not a fund of knowledge.

—John Kluge

You reach a point where you don't work for money.

—Walt Disney

If a man has wealth, he has to make a choice, because there is the money heaping up. He can keep it together in a bunch, and then leave it for others to administer after he is dead. Or he can get into action and have fun, while he is still alive. I prefer getting into action and adapting it to human needs, and making the plan work.

—George Eastman

Rich Palm Beach clients all wanted the same kind of different thing.

—Billy Baldwin

The rich don't exploit the poor. They just out-compete them.

—David Brooks

Unless you choose to do great things with it, it makes no difference how much you are rewarded, or how much power you have.

—Oprah Winfrey

Having money is rather like being a blond. It is more fun but not vital.

—Mary Quant

I just lucked into things. I used to think that if
I made $50,000 I'd be the happiest guy in the world.

—Kirk Kerkorian

The more you own, the more you know you don't own.

—Aristotle Onassis

The greatest good we can do for others is not
just to share our riches with them, but to reveal theirs.

—Zig Ziglar

The property boom has made us all feel wealthy,
but unfortunately it has lulled many of those
nearing retirement into a false sense of security.

—Noel Whittaker

Over a three-year period, I gave away half of what I had. To be honest, my hands shook as I signed it away. I knew I was taking myself out of the race to be the richest man in the world.

—Ted Turner

Fortunes are made, and disappear, over the lifetime of a single generation. Today, a person in essence takes his wealth from society just for the duration of his or her lifetime. The next generation has to create it anew.

—Mikhail Khodorkovsky

What do I care about law? Ain't I got the power?

—Cornelius Vanderbilt

Let me tell you about the very rich. They are different from you and me. They possess and enjoy early, and it does something to them, makes them soft where we are hard, cynical where we are trustful, in a way that, unless you were born rich, it is very difficult to understand.

—F. Scott Fitzgerald (who never said the line that is widely attributed to him: "The rich are different than you and me—they have more money.")

The rich are different from you and me because they have more credit.

—John Leonard

Having money is just the best thing in the world.

—Madonna

I had to get rich to see being rich is not important.

—Tom Monaghan

You know, gentlemen, that I do not owe any personal income tax. But nevertheless, I send a small check, now and then, to the Internal Revenue Service out of the kindness of my heart.

—David Rockefeller

I can hire one half of the working class to kill the other half.

—Jay Gould

As men get older, the toys get more expensive.

—Marvin Davis

Give money me, take friendship whoso list,
For friends are gone come once adversity.
When money yet remaineth safe in chest,
That quickly can thee bring from misery.
Fair face show friends when riches do abound;

—Barnabe Googe

The secret point of money and power in America is neither the things that money can buy nor power for power's sake . . . but absolute personal freedom, mobility, privacy.

—Joan Didion

If wealth is found by rejecting the experience of poverty, then it will never be complete.

—Dr. Thomas Moore

Money is human happiness in the abstract: he, then, who is no longer capable of enjoying human happiness in the concrete devotes his heart entirely to money.

—Arthur Schopenhauer

Money is only congealed snow.

—Dorothy Parker

I'm not doing my philanthropic work, out of any kind of guilt, or any need to create good public relations. I'm doing it because I can afford to do it, and I believe in it.

—George Soros

Loco Dempsey: I wouldn't mind marrying a Vanderbilt.
Pola Debevoise: Or Mr. Cadillac.
Schatze Page: No such person. I checked.
Loco Dempsey: Is there a Mr. Texaco?

—from the film *How to Marry a Millionaire*

Money's a horrid thing to follow, but a charming thing to meet.

—Henry James, *The Portrait of a Lady*

Money gives me pleasure all the time.

—Hilaire Belloc

Money is better than poverty, if only for financial reasons.

—Woody Allen

Probably the very best thing my earnings have given me is absense of worry. I have not forgotten what it feels like to worry whether you'll have enough to pay the bills. Not to have to think about that any more is the biggest luxury in the world.

—J. K. Rowling

If I go to a match, it doesn't mean I want to buy the stadium or the club.

—Lakshmi Mittal

Money has no moral opinions.

—from the film *Force Of Evil*

If you owe the bank $100, that's your problem.
If you owe the bank $100 million, that's the bank's problem.

—J. Paul Getty

Whatever qualities the rich may have, they can be acquired by anyone with the tenacity to become rich. The key, I think, is confidence. Confidence and an unshakable belief it can be done and that you are the one to do it.

—Felix Dennis

Money itself isn't lost or made, it's simply transferred from one perception to another. This painting here. I bought it 10 years ago for 60 thousand dollars. I could sell it today for 600. The illusion has become real and the more real it becomes, the more desperately they want it.

—from the film *Wall Street*

If you have millions of dollars it changes your lifestyle, and anyone who says differently is talking bullshit. I don't need to work, from a standard of living point of view, but I do, you know. I work every day and on weekends and I haven't taken a vacation for years.

—Elon Musk

Money is that dear thing which,
if you're not careful, you can squander
your whole life thinking of. . . .

—Mary Jo Salter

Money, which represents the prose of life, and which is hardly spoken of in parlors without an apology, is, in its effects and laws, as beautiful as roses.

—Ralph Waldo Emerson

If women didn't exist, all the money in the world would have no meaning.

—Aristotle Onassis

Being rich is having money. Being wealthy is having time.

—Stephen Swid

Where large sums of money are concerned, it is advisable to trust nobody.

—Agatha Christie

Money isn't everything . . . but it ranks right up there with oxygen.

—Rita Davenport

If you have more money than you need, you have to give it away. It's a duty. I get to choose whom to sponsor, and I like to give to the areas that I know something about.

—Gordon Getty

Even though money seems such an objective topic, it can also be the most intimate, and possibly harmful, part of a relationship.

—Christie Hefner

In bad times, the rich usually get richer.

—Stuart Wilde

I've never been poor. Being poor is a state of mind. Being broke is only a temporary situation.

—Mike Todd

One must choose, in life, between making money and spending it. There's no time to do both.

—Edouard Bourdet

The darkest hour of any man's life is when he sits down to plan how to get money without earning it.

—Horace Greely

Money, says the proverb, makes money. When you have got a little, it is often easy to get more.

—Charles Dickens

If a man runs after money, he's money-mad; if he keeps it, he's a capitalist; if he spends it, he's a playboy; if he doesn't get it, he's a ne'er-do-well; if he doesn't try to get it, he lacks ambition. If he gets it without working for it, he's a parasite; and if he accumulates it after a lifetime of hard work, people call him a fool who never got anything out of life.

—Vic Oliver

Money is a kind of poetry.

—Wallace Stevens

Man is a money-making animal, which propensity too often interferes with his benevolence.

—Herman Melville

The lover of money will not be satisfied with money; nor the lover of wealth, with gain.

—The Old Testament, Ecclesiastes 5:10

There are but three modes in which surplus wealth can be disposed of. It call be left to the families of the decedents; or it can be bequeathed for public purposes; or, finally, it can be administered during their lives by its possessors.

—Andrew Carnegie, "The Gospel of Wealth"

If a man has money, it is usually a sign, too, that he knows how to take care of it; don't imagine his money is easy to get simply because he has plenty of it.

—Edgar Watson Howe

Capital as such is not evil; it is its wrong use that is evil. Capital in some form or other will always be needed.

—Mohandas K. Gandhi

Many people think that by hoarding money they are gaining safety for themselves. If money is your *only* hope for independence, you will never have it. The only real security that a person can have in this world is a reserve of knowledge, experience, and ability. Without these qualities, money is practically useless.

—Henry Ford

He that is of the opinion money will do everything may well be suspected of doing everything for money.

—Benjamin Franklin

I was part of that strange race of people aptly described as spending their lives doing things they detest to make money they don't want to buy things they don't need to impress people they dislike.

—Emile Henry Gauvreau

Sex is like money; only too much is enough.

—John Updike

The perfect pleasure: money is neither fattening nor immoral nor illegal.

—Mason Cooley

Nothing lulls and inebriates like money; when you have a lot, the world seems a better place than it actually is.

—Anton Chekhov

The lesson of value which money teaches, which the Author of the Universe has taken so much pains to teach us, we are inclined to skip altogether.

—Henry David Thoreau

My boy . . . always try to rub up against money, for if you rub up against money long enough, some of it may rub off on you.

—Damon Runyon

I have the disadvantage of not being sociable. Wall Street men are fond of company and sport. A man makes one hundred thousand dollars there and immediately buys a yacht, begins to race fast horses, and becomes a sport generally. My tastes lie in a different direction. When business hours are over I go home and spend the remainder of the day with my wife, my children, and books of my library. Every man has natural inclinations of his own. Mine are domestic. They are not calculated to make me particularly popular in Wall Street, and I cannot help that.

—Jay Gould

There are two things necessary to Salvation . . . money and gunpowder.

—George Bernard Shaw, *Major Barbara*

Get place and wealth, if possible, with grace;
if not, by any means get wealth and place.

—Alexander Pope

Money is power, and you ought to be reasonably ambitious to have it.

—Russell Herman Conwell

I'm tired of Love; I'm still more tired of Rhyme.
But money gives me pleasure all the time.

—Hillaire Belloc

I buy newspapers to make money to buy more newspapers to make more money.

—Lord Thompson of Fleet

Weapons are like money; no one knows the meaning of enough.

—Martin Amis

Preoccupation with money is the great test of small natures, but only a small test of great ones.

—Sébastien-Roch Nicolas De Chamfort

Yes! Ready money is Aladdin's lamp.

—Lord Byron

You can be young without money but you can't be old without it.

—Tennessee Williams, *Cat on a Hot Tin Roof*

I am only interested in money because everyone else is.

—Mason Cooley

The truth is, there is money buried everywhere, and you have only to go to work to find it.

—Henry David Thoreau

Business, you know, may bring money,
but friendship hardly ever does.

—Jane Austen

Capital is money, capital is commodities. . . . By virtue of it being value, it has acquired the occult ability to add value to itself. It brings forth living offspring, or, at the least, lays golden eggs.

—Karl Marx

The best thing you can do for the poor is not to be one of them.

—Frederick "Reverend Ike" Eikerenkootter

When it comes to money, nobody should give up anything.

—Anthony Trollope

Banking was conceived in iniquity and was born in sin. The Bankers own the earth. Take it away from them, but leave them the power to create deposits, and with the flick of the pen they will create enough deposits to buy it back again. However, take it away from them, and all the great fortunes like mine will disappear and they ought to disappear, for this would be a happier and better world to live in. But, if you wish to remain the slaves of Bankers and pay the cost of your own slavery, let them continue to create deposits.

—Sir Josiah Stamp

The day is not far distant when the man who dies leaving behind him millions of available wealth, which was free for him to administer during life, will pass away unwept, unhonored, and unsung, no matter to what uses he leave the dross which he cannot take with him. Of such as these the public verdict will then be: The man who dies thus rich dies disgraced.

—Andrew Carnegie

To me, money is a means to do good. I reached a point in my life where I had enjoyed tremendous business success that afforded my family everything we could possibly want. My wife and I then decided that we could use our wealth to make a difference. So we created the Broad Foundations to do four things: to improve urban public education, to support innovative scientific and medical research, to foster art appreciation for audiences worldwide, and to support civic initiatives in Los Angeles.

—Eli Broad

There are plenty of ways to get ahead. The first is so basic I'm almost embarrassed to say it: Spend less than you earn.

—Paul Clitheroe

The bottom line is that if I did it, you can do it. I got rich without the benefit of a college education or a penny of capital but making many errors along the way. I went from being a pauper—a hippie dropout on the dole, living in a crummy room without the proverbial pot to piss in, without even the money to pay the rent, without a clue as to what to do next—to being rich . . .

—Felix Dennis

A nation is not in danger of financial disaster merely because it owes itself money.

—Andrew W. Melon

Excess of wealth is cause of covetousness.

—Christopher Marlowe, *The Jew of Malta*

All this [wealth] excludes but one evil—poverty.

—Samuel Johnson

Those that have wealth must be watchful and wary, Power, alas! naught but misery brings.

—Thomas Haynes Bayly

. . . the man of wealth thus becoming the mere agent and trustee for his poorer brethren, bringing to their service his superior wisdom, experience and ability to administer, doing for them better than they would or could do for themselves.

—Andrew Carnegie, "The Gospel of Wealth"

Ill fares the land, to hastening ills a prey,
where wealth accumulates, and men decay.

—Oliver Goldsmith, *The Deserted Village*

No one goes to Hades with all his immense wealth.

—Theognis

If you leave the labor force thinking you have plenty, and then realize that you don't, then you are stuck.

—Robert Friedland

Lampis, the sea commander, being asked how he got his wealth, answered, "My greatest estate I gained easily enough, but the smaller slowly and with much labour."

—Plutarch

It is once your ideas have been transformed into enough money, and if all failed, you would still live your lifestyle, and you understand that just because you have made more money than most, you are not better than the common person. We are all going to die broke.

—Tim Blixseth on what "success" is to him

The boast of heraldry, the pomp of pow'r,
And all that beauty, all that wealth e'er gave,
Await alike the inevitable hour.
The paths of glory lead but to the grave.

—Thomas Gray, *Elegy in a Country Churchyard*

I would as soon leave my son a curse as the almighty dollar.

—Andrew Carnegie

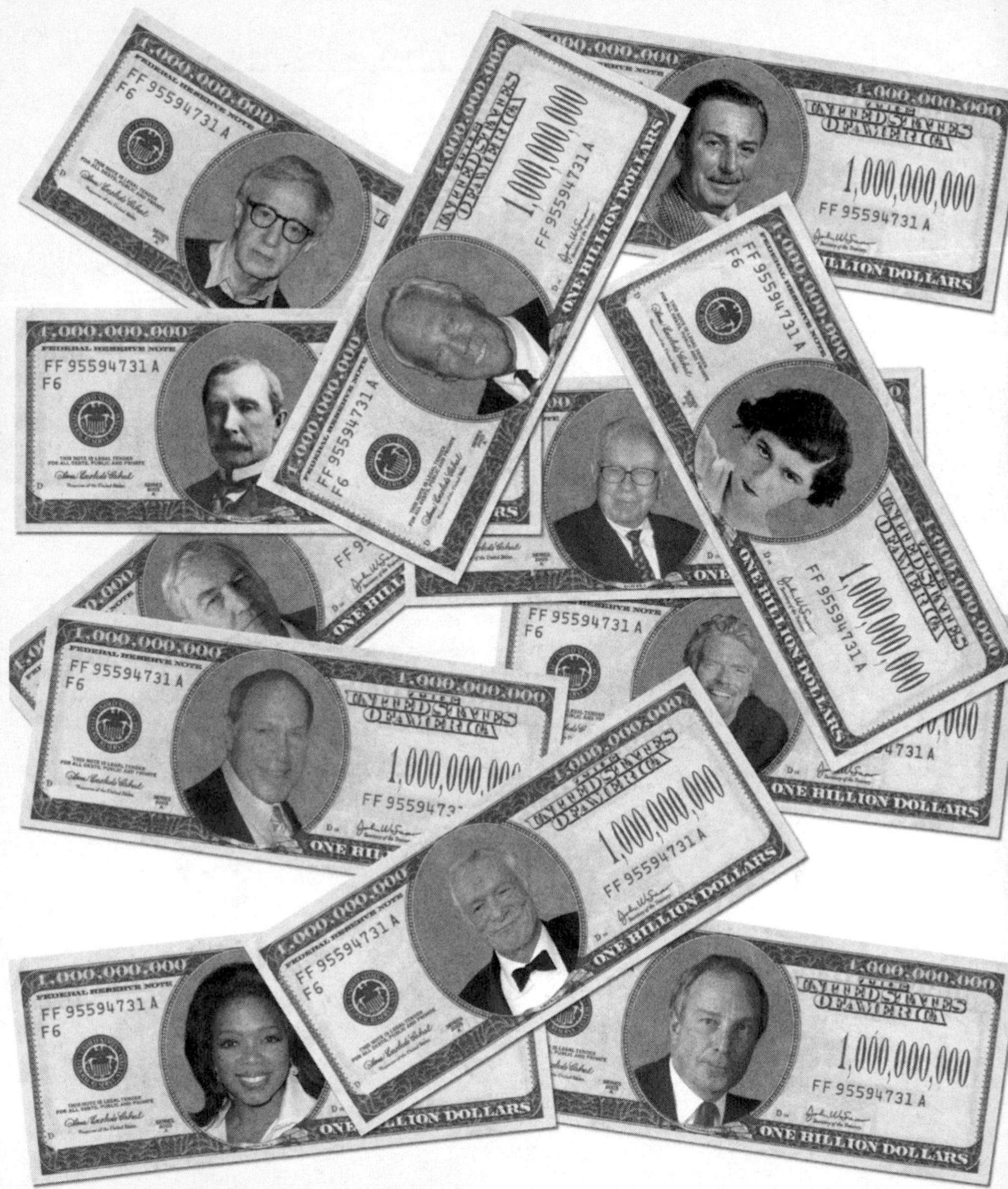

2

Goals

1,000,000,000
FEDERAL RESERVE NOTE
FF 95594731 A
F6
THE UNITED STATES OF AMERICA
1,000,000,000
FF 95594731 A
ONE BILLION DOLLARS

If your only goal is to become rich,
you will never achieve it.

—John D. Rockefeller

Give me a stock clerk with a goal and I'll give you a man who will make history. Give me a man with no goals and I'll give you a stock clerk.

—James Cash Penny

To succeed in business it is necessary to make others see things as you see them.

—Aristotle Onassis

The goal is to win. It's not about making money. I have many much less risky ways of making money than this (buying Chelsea football club). I don't want to throw my money away, but it's really about having fun and that means success and trophies.

—Roman Abramovich

Having an aim is the key to achieving your best.

—Henry J. Kaiser

The entire essence of America is the hope to first make money—then make money with money—then make lots of money with lots of money.

—Paul Erdman

The most successful businessman is the man who holds onto the old just as long as it is good, and grabs the new just as soon as it is better.

—Lee Iococca

Take the pains required to become what you want to become, or you might end up becoming something you'd rather not be. That is also a daily discipline and worth considering.

—Donald Trump

It is better to aim at perfection and miss it than to aim at imperfection and hit it.

—Thomas Watson

Basically, our goal is to organize the world's information and to make it universally accessible and useful.

—Larry Page

The main object in view is to train young men to useful trades and occupations, so that they can earn their own livelihood.

—Milton Hershey

A company that feels it has reached its goal will quickly stagnate and lose its vitality.

—Ingvar Kamprad

What matters is where you want to go. Focus in the right direction!

—Donald Trump

Twenty years and $40 billion.
They seem like good round numbers.

—Michael Dell

We wanted Nike to be the world's best sports and fitness company. Once you say that, you have a focus. You don't end up making wing tips or sponsoring the next Rolling Stones world tour.

—Philip Knight

The older I get, the more I see a straight path where I want to go. If you're going to hunt elephants, don't get off the trail for a rabbit.

—T. Boone Pickens

A corporation's primary goal is to make money. Government's primary role is to take a big chunk of that money and give it to others.

—Larry Ellison

3

Secrets of Success

Formula for success: rise early, work hard, strike oil.

—J. Paul Getty

I do not think that there is any other quality so essential to success of any kind as the quality of perseverance. It overcomes almost everything, even nature.

—John D. Rockefeller

It's a proprietary strategy. I can't go into it in great detail.

—Bernard Madoff

Success is not about doing things well or even very well, or being acknowledged by others. It is not an external opinion, but rather an internal status. It is the harmony between the soul and your emotions, which requires love, family, friendship, authenticity and integrity.

—Carlos Slim Helú

I believe the true road to preeminent success in any line is to make yourself master in that line. I have no faith in the policy of scattering one's resources, and in my experience I have rarely if ever met a man who achieved preeminence in money making—certainly never one in manufacturing—who was interested in many concerns.

—Andrew Carnegie

I have had all of the disadvantages required for success.

—Larry Ellison

Success is often achieved by those who don't know that failure is inevitable.

—Coco Chanel

Obviously everyone wants to be successful, but I want to be looked back on as being very innovative, very trusted and ethical, and ultimately making a big difference in the world.

—Sergey Brin

No man can climb the ladder of success without first placing his foot on the bottom rung.

—James Cash Penny

There is an immutable conflict at work in life and in business, a constant battle between peace and chaos. Neither can be mastered, but both can be influenced. How you go about that is the key to success.

—Philip Knight

There is no scientific answer for success.
You can't define it. You've simply got to live it and do it.

—Anita Roddick

The size of your success is measured by the strength of your desire, the size of your dream, and how you handle disappointment along the way.

—Robert Kiyosaki

To do a common thing uncommonly well brings success.

—Henry J. Heinz

The successful team is the one that makes 1 plus 1 equal 11.

—Mohammad bin Rashid Al Maktoum

Reputation is the key to success. You have to be loyal to your customers.

—Li Ka-shing

What's the secret to success? It's no secret. You need a winning attitude, honesty and integrity, and a burning desire to succeed.

—Dave Thomas

The man who has done his level best, and who is conscious that he has done his best, is a success, even though the world may write him down as a failure.

—Bertie Charles Forbes

There is no substitute for knowledge. To this day, I read three newspapers a day. It is impossible to read a paper without being exposed to ideas. And ideas . . . more than money . . . are the real currency for success.

—Eli Broad

There is no royal flower-strewn path to success. And if there is, I have not found it for if I have accomplished anything in life it is because I have been willing to work hard.

—Madam C. J. Walker

There are a lot of things that go into creating success. I don't like to do just the things I like to do. I like to do things that cause the company to succeed. I don't spend a lot of time doing my favorite activities.

—Michael Dell

Overcoming hardships and working around and through their obstacles to achieve an education is what I call a true success.

—Wayne Huizeaga

Willpower is the key to success. Successful people strive no matter what they feel by applying their will to overcome apathy, doubt, or fear.

—Dan Millman

The key to success is to get out into the store and listen to what the associates have to say. It's terribly important for everyone to get involved. Our best ideas come from clerks and stockboys.

—Sam Walton

The most successful businessman is the man who holds onto the old just as long as it is good, and grabs the new just as soon as it is better.

—Lee Iococca

My success wasn't based on how I could push down everyone around me. My success was based on how much I could push everybody up . . . And in the process they pushed me up, and I pushed them up, and we kept doing that, and we still do that.

—George Lucas

No one can possibly achieve any real and lasting success or get rich in business by being a conformist.

—J. Paul Getty

Success in business requires training and discipline and hard work. But if you're not frightened by these things, the opportunities are just as great today as they ever were.

—David Rockefeller

The secret of my success is a two-word answer: Know people.

—Harvey S. Firestone

If life was so easy that you could just go buy success, there would be a lot more successful companies in the world. Successful enterprises are built from the ground up.

—Louis V. Gerstner

The turning point, I think, was when I really realized that you can do it yourself. That you have to believe in you because sometimes that's the only person that does believe in your success but you.

—Tim Blixseth

Recognize that there will be failures, and acknowledge that there will be obstacles. But you will learn from your mistakes and the mistakes of others, for there is very little learning in success.

—Michael Dell

The jests of the rich are ever successful.

—Oliver Goldsmith

And make sure that capital structure we have in place is the right capital structure. I think that's the reason that we've been successful.

—Henry Kravis

The secret of success is to do common things uncommonly well.

—John D. Rockefeller

The successful person makes a habit of doing what the failing person doesn't like to do.

—Thomas Edison

If there is any one secret of success, it lies in the ability to get the other person's point of view and see things from that person's angle as well as from your own.

—Henry Ford

I can't give you any secret recipe for success, any foolproof plan for making it in the world of business. But my own experience suggests that it is possible to start from nothing and achieve even beyond your dreams.

—Howard Schultz

I never thought I'd be successful. It seems in my own mind that in everything I've undertaken I've never quite made the mark. But I've always been able to put disappointments aside. Success isn't about the end result; it's about what you learn along the way.

—Vera Wang

I didn't become a successful businessman because I wanted to be rich and famous. I wanted to become successful enough to deliver the art to the consumer.

—Todd McFarlane

A business is successful to the extent that it provides a product or service that contributes to happiness in all of its forms.

—Mihaly Csikszentmihalyi

People are what determine your success in the future. Surround yourself with good people and you won't fail.

—Wayne Huizenga

You can't have a clean floor with a dirty mop bucket. To be successful, you need to take care of the basics of your business—and that means making sure you don't overlook the little details.

—Dave Thomas

I have found no greater satisfaction than achieving success through honest dealing and strict adherence to the view that, for you to gain, those you deal with should gain as well.

—Alan Greenspan

My life experience tells me that success is never final, but the decisions we make along the way determine the end and final outcome.

—J. Willard Marriott

The core of our success, that's the most difficult thing for a competitor to imitate. They can buy all the physical things. The things you can't buy are dedication, devotion, loyalty—the feeling that you are participating in a crusade.

—Herb Kelleher

We're never arrogant, we're always looking at the competition. But they have not been successful for a couple of reasons. The intent to socialize on a site like Yahoo! isn't really there because the brand doesn't necessarily stand for anything and there's no real voice to it.

—Tom Anderson and Chris De Wolfe

If you're successful in business it's because you've served other people; you've served your employees; you've served your customers. You're creating jobs.

—Tom Monaghan

Singleness of purpose is one of the chief essentials for success in life, no matter what may be one's aim.

—John D. Rockefeller

Whatever it is that you're successful at, that has to be the number one goal. In my case, it's accessibility. So all of my products have to be usable, accessible, affordable.

—Rachel Ray

We measured our success not just by how much money we made, but by how much we contributed to the community. It was a two-part bottom line.

—Ben Cohen

If I had to select one quality, one personal characteristic that I regard as being most highly correlated with success, whatever the field, I would pick the trait of persistence . . . The will to endure to the end, to get knocked down seventy times and get up off the floor saying, "Here comes number seventy-one!"

—Richard M. DeVos

If you want to succeed you should strike out on new paths, rather than travel the worn paths of accepted success.

—John D. Rockefeller

We accept criticism because it leads us to the right path. All humans err. A successful man, in my opinion, may err twice, but he will succeed eight times.

—Mohammad bin Rashid Al Maktoum

Failure is success if we learn from it.

—Malcolm S. Forbes

Enjoy failure and learn from it.
You can never learn from success.

—Sir James Dyson

Whenever you see a successful business, someone once made a courageous decision.

—Peter Drucker

Success seems to be connected with action. Successful people keep moving. They make mistakes, but they don't quit.

—Conrad Hilton

4

Entrepreneurs and Enterprise

If you wait until all the lights are green before you leave home, you'll never get started on your trip to the top.

—Zig Ziglar

I got my start by giving myself a start.

—Madam C. J. Walker

If you have ideas, you have the main asset you need, and there isn't any limit to what you can do with your business and your life. Ideas are any man's greatest asset.

—Harvey S. Firestone

As I stood there with the razor in my hand, my eyes resting on it as lightly as a bird settling down on its nest, the Gillette razor was born. In that moment I saw it all: the way the blade could be held in a holder; the idea of sharpening the two opposite edges on the thin piece of steel; the clamping plates, with a handle halfway between the two edges of the blade.

—King Gillette

The five essential entrepreneurial skills for success: Concentration, Discrimination, Organization, Innovation, and Communication.

—Harold S. Geneen

The man who comes up with a means for doing or producing almost anything better, faster or more economically has his future and his fortune at his fingertips.

—J. Paul Getty

Watch the turtle. He only moves forward by sticking his neck out.

—Louis V. Gerstner

The most important thing for a young man is to establish a credit . . . a reputation, character.

—John D. Rockefeller

It is true that there is a fine line between entrepreneurship and insanity. Crazy people see and feel things that others don't. But you have to believe that everything is possible. If you believe it, those around you will believe it too.

—Anita Roddick

That's one thing about me. I'm my own businessman. I'm my own person. The team I built taught me how to get into business, how to run a business. They gave me the knowledge I needed to have. But now I'm on my own.

—Ervin "Magic" Johnson

I wanted to be an editor or a journalist, I wasn't really interested in being an entrepreneur, but I soon found I had to become an entrepreneur in order to keep my magazine going.

—Richard Branson

You can never be comfortable with your success, you've got to be paranoid you're going to lose it.

—Louis V. Gerstner

Decide what you want, decide what you are willing to exchange for it. Establish your priorities and go to work.

—H. L. Hunt

Failure is simply the opportunity to begin again, this time more intelligently.

—Henry Ford

If you hesitate, some bolder hand will stretch out before you and get the prize.

—Phineas T. Barnum

Somehow I can't believe there are any heights that can't be scaled by a man who knows the secret of making dreams come true. This special secret, it seems to me, can be summarized in four Cs. They are Curiosity, Confidence, Courage, and Constancy and the greatest of these is Confidence.

—Walt Disney

When I work fourteen hours a day, seven days a week, I get lucky.

—Armand Hammer

Much good work is lost for the lack of a little more.

—Edward H. Harriman

Live daringly, boldly, fearlessly. Taste the relish to be found in competition—in having put forth the best within you.

—Henry J. Kaiser

The most important piece of advice that I could give [people starting out] is to take advantage of the tremendous reservoir of knowledge that's out there today. Spend some time learning how the world has evolved. There are a lot of good lessons in history, and other peoples' experiences in the past, that could be exactly the solution to the problem you're looking for.

—Frederick W. Smith

The idea of an entrepreneur is really thinking out of the box and taking risks and stepping up to major challenges. You can be entrepreneurial even if you don't want to be in business.

—Steve Case

If you don't have daily objectives, you qualify as a dreamer.

—Zig Ziglar

You've got to start with your gut, with something you are really passionate about, for a good reason. You won't get there by sitting in a closet and thinking, "Boy I know the world must want this."

—Charles Schwab

Capital isn't scarce; vision is.

—Sam Walton

A business absolutely devoted to service will have only one worry about profits. They will be embarrassingly large.

—Henry Ford

One of the biggest lessons I've learned recently is that when you don't know what to do, you should do nothing until you figure out what to do because a lot of times you feel like you are pressed against the wall, and you've got to make a decision. You never have to do anything. Don't know what to do? Do nothing.

—Oprah Winfrey

The greatest real thrill that life offers is to create, to construct, to develop something useful.

Too often we fail to recognize and pay tribute to the creative spirit. It is that spirit that creates our jobs.

—Alfred P. Sloan

The way to get started is to quit talking and begin doing.

—Walt Disney

You can do so much in 10 minutes' time. Ten minutes, once gone, are gone for good. Divide your life into 10-minute units and sacrifice as few of them as possible in meaningless activity.

—Ingvar Kamprad

In life and business, there are two cardinal sins . . . The first is to act precipitously without thought and the second is to not act at all.

—Carl Icahn

It has been my observation that most people get ahead during the time that others waste time.

—Henry Ford

Fear of failure must never be a reason not to try something.

—Frederick W. Smith

Always think outside the box and embrace opportunities that appear, wherever they might be.

—Lakshmi Mittal

Work eight hours and sleep eight hours and make sure that they are not the same hours.

—T. Boone Pickens

The person that turns over the most rocks wins the game. And that's always been my philosophy.

—Peter Lynch

Whatever the mind of man can conceive and believe, it can achieve. Thoughts are things! And powerful things at that, when mixed with definiteness of purpose, and burning desire, can be translated into riches.

—Napoleon Hill

The key is falling in love with something, anything. If your heart's attached to it, then your mind will be attached to it. When you have a passion for something then you tend not only to be better at it, but you work harder at it too.

—Vera Wang

I learned to embrace risk, as long as it was well thought out and, in a worst-case scenario, I'd still land on my feet.

—Eli Broad

Everything we would ever need to become rich and powerful and sophisticated is within our reach. The major reason that so few take advantage of all that we have is simply, neglect.

—Jim Rohn

The way of the pioneer is always rough.

—Harvey S. Firestone

How do you teach obsession, because more often than not it's obsession that drives an entrepreneur's vision? Why would you march to a different drumbeat if you are instinctively part of the crowd?

—Anita Roddick

Learn how to be a loser, because it's important to be a loser to be a winner.

—Sanford I. Weil

I learned that we can do anything, but we can't do everything . . . at least not at the same time. So think of your priorities not in terms of what activities you do, but when you do them. Timing is everything.

—Dan Millman

If you have a dream, give it a chance to happen.

—Richard M. DeVos

You have to have a great tolerance for pain! You have to work so hard and have so much enthusiasm for one thing that most other things in your life have to be sacrificed.

—Howard Schultz

There has to be this pioneer, the individual who has the courage, the ambition to overcome the obstacles that always develop when one tries to do something worthwhile, especially when it is new and different.

—Alfred P. Sloan

The lesson here is that if you want to get really rich, go into business for yourself. In a capitalistic society, the biggest rewards go to capitalists, not to managers.

—Theodore Waitt

Don't worry about it. Babe Ruth struck out on occasion, too.

—Walter Annenberg

There are always opportunities through which businessmen can profit handsomely if they will only recognize and seize them.

—J. Paul Getty

The best route to the top is to own the company.

—Lewis Bookwalter Ward

You know, sometimes people never get to learn how successful they could have been because they give up too easily.

—Russell Simmons

I believe that women entrepreneurship and innovation are not only opportunities for personal financial growth but can be vehicles to bring about positive change in our communities, to eliminate poverty.

—Sheila C. Johnson

The long and short of it for me is that the entrepreneur is the one who at the end decides yes or no and I like that even though it's a lot of responsibility.

—Giorgio Armani

Starting and growing a business is as much about the innovation, drive, and determination of the people who do it as it is about the product they sell.

—Elon Musk

Time is our most precious asset, we should invest it wisely.

—Michael Levy

I want to see how it works. If it doesn't work, then I'll use the same line that Steve Jobs uses: "Sometimes when you innovate, you make mistakes."

—Peter van Stolk

I had to make my own living and my own opportunity. But I made it! Don't sit down and wait for the opportunities to come. Get up and make them.

—Madam C. J. Walker

Forget about the pie in the sky, get yours here and now.

—Frederick "Reverend Ike" Eikerenkootter

I'm an entrepreneur. I like building companies, but I also like building projects. The question for me is how do you get more change, more out-of-the-box thinking, and more focused on scaling in the charitable sector.

—Steve Case

Coming together is a beginning. Keeping together is progress. Working together is success.

—Henry Ford

There was nothing on the market that I felt was any good, so I decided to make something myself.

—Julie Aigner

Ability will never catch up with the demand for it.

—Malcolm S. Forbes

Good timber does not grow with ease.
The stronger the wind, the stronger the trees.

—J. Willard Marriott

It's all to do with the training: you can do a lot if you're properly trained.

—Queen Elizabeth II

Before you try to convince anyone else, be sure you are convinced, and if you cannot convince yourself, drop the subject.

—John Henry Patterson

Don't limit yourself. Many people limit themselves to what they think they can do. You can go as far as your mind lets you. What you believe, remember, you can achieve.

—Mary Kay Ash

If you're not a risk taker, you should get the hell out of business.

—Ray Kroc

I have found that I always learn more from my mistakes than from my successes. If you aren't making some mistakes, you aren't taking enough chances.

—John Sculley

Engage in one kind of business only, and stick to it faithfully until you succeed, or until your experience shows that you should abandon it.

—Phineas T. Barnum

[We stop growing] if we start being afraid of taking risks and if we start diminishing our creative pertinence. We should always aim at doing more-creative endeavors, not in terms of volume but in terms of more creativity and more sharing.

—Guy Laliberte

Toil and production are two distinguishing characteristics of a creative man.

—Mohammad bin Rashid Al Maktoum

A major stimulant to creative thinking is focused questions. There is something about a well-worded question that often penetrates to the heart of the matter and triggers new ideas and insights.

—Brian Tracy

Capital isn't that important in business. Experience isn't that important. You can get both of these things. What is important is ideas.

—Harvey S. Firestone

I've heard of Monday, Tuesday, Wednesday, Thursday, and Friday. But I've never heard of Someday.

—Frederick "Reverend Ike" Eikerenkootter

Whether you've found your calling, or if you're still searching, passion should be the fire that drives your life's work.

—Michael Dell

When we started Google, we thought "Oh, we might fail," and we almost didn't do it. We had all this internal risk that we had just invented . . . fear of failing and doing something new . . . In order to do stuff that matters, you need to overcome that.

—Larry Page

It is impossible to win the race unless you venture to run, impossible to win the victory unless you dare to battle.

—Richard M. DeVos

Most people spend more time and energy going around problems than in trying to solve them.

—Henry Ford

When you lose small businesses, you lose big ideas. People who own their own businesses are their own bosses. They are independent thinkers. They know they can't compete by imitating the big guys; they have to innovate. So they are less obsessed with earnings than they are with ideas.

—Ted Turner

Don't bunt. Aim out of the ball park.
Aim for the company of immortals.

—David Ogilvy

When I started eBay, it was a hobby, an experiment to see if people could use the Internet to be empowered through access to an efficient market. I actually wasn't thinking about it in terms of a social impact. It was really about helping people connect around a sphere of interest so they could do business.

—Pierre Omidyar

First, I see what is needed in the marketplace. The next thing is I ask what's out there. What you don't want to do is come up with a product and then find out that someone is successfully marketing a good product and can take business away.

—Ron Popeil

Do not wait; the time will never be just right. Start where you stand, and work with whatever tools you may have at your command, and better tools will be found as you go along.

—Napoleon Hill

Vision is perhaps our greatest strength . . . it has kept us alive to the power and continuity of thought through the centuries, it makes us peer into the future and lends shape to the unknown.

—Li Ka-shing

Start out with an ideal and end up with a deal.

—Karl Albrecht

If you're going to succeed in growing market share, you need to have the product on the shelf, . . . Our strategy is to be in stock and provide real value for consumers. The last thing we want to do is pass up an opportunity to take advantage of a trend we see taking place in our stores.

—Richard Schulze

If the specialist cannot effectively perform his role, then we need to look for alternatives including the electronic matching of buyers and sellers, with no human intervention.

—Maurice Greenberg

And learn that when you do make a mistake, you'll surface that mistake so you can get it corrected, rather than trying to hide it and bury it, and it becomes a much bigger mistake, and maybe a fatal mistake.

—Sanford I. Weill

I swore I was going to exclusively collect assets and not liabilities for the rest of my life. I swore never to take gambles I couldn't back up, or that I couldn't afford to lose. And, I've stuck with that ever since.

—Tim Blixseth

I am an extreme optimist, while [my husband] likes to play the devil's advocate. He wants to know the worst thing that can happen. I don't even want to think about the worst case. I provide the discipline and stick-to-it-iveness.

—Jenny Craig

If I had some idea of a finish line, don't you think I would have crossed it years ago?

—Richard M. DeVos

Nothing is an obstacle unless you say it is.

—Wally Amos

I'm willing to make a serious investment in an idea and take two to two and one-half years of my life to create it, to get behind it and understand it and take it to the marketplace.

—Ron Popeil

The secret is not to give up hope. It's very hard not to because if you're really doing something worthwhile I think you will be pushed to the brink of hopelessness before you come through the other side. You just have to hang in through that.

—George Lucas

You must keep your mind on the objective, not on the obstacle.

—William Handolph Hearst

I just don't like to sit around and wait for something to happen. It's more fun making it happen.

—Joyce Hall

I had to pick myself up and get on with it,
do it all over again, only even better this time.

—Sam Walton

Go as far as you can see; when you get there, you'll be able to see farther.

—J. P. Morgan

I feel sorry for the person who can't get genuinely excited about his work. Not only will he never be satisfied, but he will never achieve anything worthwhile.

—Walter Chrysler

Endless meetings, sloppy communications, and red tape steal the entrepreneur's time.

—James L. Hayes

I never get the accountants in before I start up a business. It's done on gut feeling, especially if I can see that they are taking the mickey out of the consumer.

—Richard Branson

You can't build a reputation on what you are going to do.

—Henry Ford

Innovation is the specific tool of entrepreneurs, the means by which they exploit change as an opportunity for a different business or a different service. It is capable of being presented as a discipline, capable of being learned, capable of being practiced.

—Peter F. Drucker

Vitally important for a young man or woman is, first, to realize the value of education and then to cultivate earnestly, aggressively, ceaselessly, the habit of self-education.

—Bertie Charles Forbes

Problems are only opportunities in work clothes.

—Henry J. Kaiser

I teach something called The Law of Probabilities, which says the more things you try, the more likely one of them will work. The more books you read, the more likely one of them will have an answer to a question that could solve the major problems of your life . . . make you wealthier, solve a health problem, whatever it might be.

—Jack Canfield

Without the element of uncertainty, the bringing off of even the greatest business triumph would be dull, routine, and eminently unsatisfying.

—J. Paul Getty

Fortune cannot be flattered by such fetish worship.
But she can be wooed and won by hard work.

—Lord Beaverbrook

To me, failure is only a way of communicating that it is not working. Stop what you're doing and try something else until it works. The one thing that I think is critical in the entrepreneurial spirit is that it's all attitude. If you think you can, then you're half way there. If you say, "I can't," then you're defeated.

—Debbi Fields

In times of rapid change, experience could be your worst enemy.

—J. Paul Getty

I did something that challenged the banking world. Conventional banks look for the rich; we look for the absolutely poor. All people are entrepreneurs, but many don't have the opportunity to find that out.

—Muhammad Yunus

Many a fortune has slipped through a man's fingers because he was engaged in too many occupations at a time.

—Phineas T. Barnum

I don't think of myself as a poor, deprived ghetto girl who made good. I think of myself as somebody who from an early age knew I was responsible for myself, and I had to make good.

—Oprah Winfrey

The opportunity for an entrepreneur to start
a company from scratch today is abysmal.

—David Geffen

Those fighting for free enterprise and free competition do not defend the interests of those rich today. They want a free hand left to unknown men who will be the entrepreneurs of tomorrow . . .

—Ludwig von Mises

Entrepreneurship is the last refuge of the troublemaking individual.

—Mason Cooley

Singleness of purpose is one of the chief essentials for success in life, no matter what may be one's aim.

—John D. Rockefeller

Capitalists are motivated not chiefly by the desire to consume wealth or indulge their appetites, but by the freedom and power to consummate their entrepreneurial ideas.

—George Gilder

It is only the farmer who faithfully plants seeds in the Spring, who reaps a harvest in the Fall.

—Bertie Charles Forbes

Don't be afraid to make a mistake. But make sure you don't make the same mistake twice.

—Akio Morita

Success is the sum of details.

—Harvey S. Firestone

If a person is not willing to make a mistake, you're never going to do anything right.

—Sanford I. Weill

Rules are sometimes a problem when you're a creative entrepreneur.

—Russell Simmons

In all honesty, I wouldn't say that the business end of it came with any kind of ease. It was more Darwinian. You have to learn business if you're going to be self-employed and survive. If you're a bad businessperson and you're an entrepreneur, you're going to be out of business.

—Todd McFarlane

One of the best classes I ever took was entrepreneurship in my freshman year . . . There is much more to starting a business than just understanding finance, accounting, and marketing. Teaching kids what has worked with startup companies and learning about experiences that others have had could really make a difference.

—Mark Cuban

Don't spend so much time trying to choose the perfect opportunity that you miss the right opportunity.

—Michael Dell

Dream small dreams. If you make them too big, you get overwhelmed and you don't do anything. If you make small goals and accomplish them, it gives you the confidence to go on to higher goals.

—John Johnson

The entrepreneur is not really interested in doing the work; he is interested in creating the way the company operates. In that regard, the entrepreneur is an inventor. He or she loves to invent, but does not love to manufacture or sell or distribute what he or she invents.

—Michael Gerber

Our biggest goal is to continue to force ourselves to always start our creative work on a white page and not take advantage of past successes and challenging ourselves. I don't believe in pitfalls. I believe in taking risks and not doing the same thing twice.

—Guy Laliberte

I didn't know enough about business to realize how bad we were doing. And I didn't have the concept that you should quit at something. I can think of so many reasons why we shouldn't have made it. We were on the edge continuously.

—Fred DeLuca

If you believe that some day it's going to happen, some day it probably will happen. You just have to make sure you're there when it's happening, and ideally you're at the front of the parade, and the principle beneficiary of when it happens, but it's not a kind of thing where you just sort of sit back and wait.

—Steve Case

My father said: You must never try to make all the money that's in a deal. Let the other fellow make some money too, because if you have a reputation for always making all the money, you won't have many deals.

—J. Paul Getty

There is no better chance to train managers than in a start-up, where they have the opportunity to see the entire company as it grows.

—Gordon Moore

The critical ingredient is getting off your butt and doing something. It's as simple as that. A lot of people have ideas, but there are few who decide to do something about them now. Not tomorrow. Not next week. But today. The true entrepreneur is a doer, not a dreamer.

—Nolan Bushnell

An entrepreneur tends to bite off a little more
than he can chew hoping
he'll quickly learn how to chew it.

—Roy Ash

When you innovate, you've got to be prepared for everyone telling you you're nuts.

—Larry Ellison

But business—you have to get into the numbers, research and asking people what their needs and wants are, picking the right locations. There's a lot that goes into business. It's not just, "OK, I want to be a businessman." Boom—go with something, and hope they come in. It doesn't work like that.

—Ervin "Magic" Johnson

In business, you have an opportunity to lead and you have an opportunity to follow. Companies and entrepreneurs that are successful tend to lead.

—Peter van Stolk

When celebration of noble failure becomes institutionalized, people within the organization are more willing to reassess earlier decisions. I'm sure luck helps every successful entrepreneur. But it doesn't come [without] a lot of preparation and hard work.

—Charles Schwab

When your work speaks for itself, don't interrupt.

—Henry J. Kaiser

If you can't change your fate, change your attitude.

—Charles Revson

Waste your money and you're only out of money, but waste your time and you've lost a part of your life.

—Michael LeBoeuf

I have developer's disease. I love to sit at a drafting table and draw plans for hotels, wrestling with problems of traffic and the flow of people. That's what turns me on.

—Steve Wynn

Once you lose everything, what's the worst that's going to happen to you? You develop a self-assurance.

—Roberto Goizueta

Think. Think about your appearance, associations, actions, ambitions, accomplishment.

—Thomas Watson

Entrepreneurs are simply those who understand that there is little difference between obstacle and opportunity and are able to turn both to their advantage.

—Victor Kiam

Think not of yourself as the architect of your career but as the sculptor. Expect to have to do a lot of hard hammering and chiseling and scraping and polishing.

—Bertie Charles Forbes

Potential entrepreneurs are outsiders. They are people who imagine things as they might be, not as they are, and have the drive to change the world around them. Those are skills that business schools do not teach.

—Anita Roddick

Unfortunately, there is a flip side to having access to plentiful capital. It means that too many people without experience in building businesses have too much money.

—Henry Kravis

All I did my first year at Vogue was Xerox. But my father said to me, "Keep doing it. You're learning the business from the ground up." And he was right.

—Vera Wang

We're not afraid of risking what was our success yesterday in order to explore some new field. "We're adventurous. We like the challenge of unknown territory, unknown artistic field, and that's what stimulates us."

—Guy Laliberte

Never fear the want of business. A man who qualifies himself well for his calling never fails of employment.

—Thomas Jefferson

As I said there is nothing wrong with failing. Pick yourself up and try it again. You never are going to know how good you really are until you go out and face failure.

—Henry Kravis

The long and short of it for me is that the entrepreneur is the one who at the end decides yes or no and I like that even though it's a lot of responsibility.

—Giorgio Armani

After the idea, there is plenty of time to learn the technology.

—Sir James Dyson

If I've learned one thing in all my years in the business, it's that often things don't work out the way you want at first. But that doesn't mean you should give up. You've got to put your head down and do the work. There are no shortcuts.

—Russell Simmons

I believe, along with many others, that you must first ask for what you want before you can have it.

—Wally Amos

You have to be open-minded when those early opportunities present themselves. Take advantage of them whether they're going to make you a lot of money or not.

—Rachel Ray

Anybody can cut prices, but it takes brains to make a better article.

—Philip Armour

I never perfected an invention that I did not think about in terms of the service it might give others . . . I find out what the world needs, then I proceed to invent.

—Thomas Edison

You only have one thing to sell in life, and that's yourself.

—Henry Kravis

Quality means doing it right when no one is looking.

—Henry Ford

One worthwhile task carried to a successful conclusion is worth half-a-hundred half-finished tasks.

—Malcolm S. Forbes

When thinking about starting a business, I think it's actually better to start in a trough and come to market in a peak, than the other way around.

—Elon Musk

I think if you study—if you learn too much of what others have done, you may tend to take the same direction as everybody else.

—Milton Hershey

Surviving a failure gives you more self-confidence. Failures are great learning tools . . . but they must be kept to a minimum.

—Jeffrey Immelt

You have to schedule it. You have to plan the opportunity to think about your business and plan what you're going to do. Otherwise you're just a hamster running on a treadmill; you're never going to get anywhere. You've got to schedule it. Strategic planning is an important part of running any business and the more so for businesses that operating in multiple states and countries.

—Jim Sinegal

There is such a thing as a natural-born entrepreneur, for whom the entrepreneurial urge drives everything, and who can make a business out of almost anything. But the accidental entrepreneur like me has to fall into the opportunity or be pushed into it. Then the entrepreneurial spirit eventually catches on.

—Gordon Moore

Inside of every problem lies an opportunity.

—Robert Kiyosaki

I always tried to turn every disaster into an opportunity.

—John D. Rockefeller

For every failure, there's an alternative course of action. You just have to find it. When you come to a roadblock, take a detour.

—Mary Kay Ash

Entrepreneurs need to search purposefully for the sources of innovation, the changes and their symptoms that indicate opportunities for successful innovation. And they need to know and to apply the principles of successful innovation.

—Peter F. Drucker

If you go through life convinced that your way is always best, all the new ideas in the world will pass you by.

—Akio Morita

If you do it right 51 percent of the time you will end up a hero.

—Alfred P. Sloan

I'd love to build a company that will continue to make movies well beyond me someday. And I'd like to help start something great, even investing in it myself.

—Steven Spielberg

This world is run with far too tight a rein for luck to interfere. Fortune sells her wares; she never gives them. In some form or other, we pay for her favors; or we go empty away.

—Amelia E. Barr

I believe in being an innovator. Tomorrow can be a wonderful age.

—Walt Disney

Hard work certainly goes a long way. These days a lot of people work hard, so you have to make sure you work even harder and really dedicate yourself to what you are doing and setting out to achieve.

—Lakshmi Mittal

Many persons are always kept poor, because they are too visionary. Every project looks to them like certain successes, and therefore they keep changing from one business to another, always in hot water, always "under the harrow."

—Phineas T. Barnum

The cover-your-butt mentality of the workplace will get you only so far. The follow-your-gut mentality of the entrepreneur has the potential to take you anywhere you want to go or run you right out of business—but it's a whole lot more fun, don't you think?

—Bill Rancic

It's important to remember one thing that is essential for any entrepreneurial organization. Do what you do well. Look at other things as incremental opportunities, but don't change the basis of what you do well.

—Gordon Moore

I don't care how much power, brilliance or energy you have, if you don't harness it and focus it on a specific target, and hold it there you're never going to accomplish as much as your ability warrants.

—Zig Ziglar

Entrepreneurs are risk takers, willing to roll the dice with their money or reputation on the line in support of an idea or enterprise. They willingly assume responsibility for the success or failure of a venture and are answerable for all its facets.

—Victor Kiam

The link between my experience as an entrepreneur and that of a politician is all in one word: freedom.

—Silvio Berlusconi

Young entrepreneurs should spend an awful lot of time thinking about what they want to go into.

—John Kluge

If something doesn't work, then you know what not to do.

—Russell Simmons

Go work for somebody and get paid to learn. It's tempting to think you can go off and do your own thing, but there is so much to learn in ways you'd never know.

—Vera Wang

When you're a self-made man you start very early in life. In my case it was at nine years old when I started bringing income into the family. You get a drive that's a little different, maybe a little stronger, than somebody who inherited.

—Kirk Kerkorian

When Henry Ford made cheap, reliable cars people said, "Nah, what's wrong with a horse?" That was a huge bet he made, and it worked.

—Elon Musk

I've seen again a lot of people go through this life, who are working so hard, they wake up one day and realize that those things that they said, "I'll do that someday, I'll do that someday," well, that someday is today.

—George Lucas

The Lord will provide, but it's a good idea to give the Lord a little help.

—Joyce Hall

My son is now an entrepreneur.
That's what you're called when you don't have a job.

—Ted Turner

Believe in your dream. People may tell you that you won't make it, that you're wasting your time. If you keep your dream in mind, have done your research and are willing to work hard, you can make it come true.

—Dave Thomas

5 Leadership

Good leadership consists of showing average people how to do the work of superior people.

—John D. Rockefeller

Strong men have sound ideas and the force to make these ideas effective.

—Andrew Mellon

The primary job of leadership, and that is to create a governing purpose that unites. We do that, first of all, by establishing a meaningful goal. An overriding purpose that most people can relate to. If the goal is clear and the focus is sharp and constantly reinforced, we unify and energize through a sense of common purpose.

—Issy Sharp

When people can see which direction the leaders are going in, it becomes easier to motivate them.

—Lakshmi Mittal

My wish is that you will remember, long after this day, that an Atlanta soft-drink salesman came here to tell you that his ultimate mission wasn't to sell an extra case of Coca-Cola, but to create value over the long haul for the owners of the company he leads.

—Roberto C. Goizueta

You need to be willing to surround yourself with people more talented than you are in certain areas. You need a degree of fear of failure to keep you going. And, while everyone wants leaders who demonstrate courage, passion, and boldness, you should not be afraid to show vulnerability now and then.

—Howard Schultz

A laurel rested upon becomes wilted.

—Mary Kay Ash

I will never have a heart attack. I give them.

—George Steinbrenner

It's within everyone's grasp to become a CEO.

—Martha Stewart

Do not summon people to your office—it frightens them. Instead go to see them in their offices. This makes you visible throughout the agency. A chairman who never wanders about his agency becomes a hermit, out of touch with his staff.

—David Ogilvy

My job is to listen to ideas, maybe cook up a few of my own, and make decisions based on what's good for the shareholders and for the company.

—Philip Knight

Everybody makes business mistakes. I mean, I take the responsibility, and I did. I was the captain of the ship and I took that responsibility.

—Alan Bond

Managing directors are not paid to be busy, they are paid to think.

—Kenneth Cork

The best way to inspire people to superior performance is to convince them by everything you do and by your everyday attitude that you are wholeheartedly supporting them.

—Harold S. Geneen

One of the things I've had the advantage of, growing up and being close to the top management of this company and other companies for most of my life, is seeing how CEOs start to believe in their own infallibility. And that really scares me.

—Bill Ford, Jr.

The buck stops with the guy who signs the checks.

—Rupert Murdoch

An executive is a man who decides; sometimes he decides right, but always he decides.

—John Henry Patterson

You have to have doubts. I have collaborators I work with. I listen and then I decide. That's how it works.

—Giorgio Armani

You should have a fund of knowledge of something and out of that you make up your mind.

—John Kluge

The execution, because there are many great ideas, but you must be able to execute to succeed. It's like being the quarterback on the team or the head coach. You pick your players, develop the game plan and together, you must execute.

—Wayne Huizenga, when asked what's more important: the ideas or the execution

When we decide to do something, we do it quickly.

—Carlos Slim Helú

A lot of people are afraid to tell the truth, to say no. That's where toughness comes into play. Toughness is not being a bully. It's having backbone.

—Robert Kiyosaki

Whenever you see a successful business, someone once made a courageous decision.

—Peter Drucker

Good business leaders create a vision, articulate the vision, passionately own the vision, and relentlessly drive it to completion.

—John Welch

I want to be remembered as one of the great CEOs of our time and of my generation. And I think that I'm gonna make them proud. That's my plan.

—Dov Charney

Uncertainty will always be part of the taking-charge process.

—Harold S. Geneen

Outstanding leaders go out of their way to boost the self-esteem of their personnel. If people believe in themselves, it's amazing what they can accomplish.

—Sam Walton

All companies of any size have to continue to push to make sure you get the right leaders, the right team, the right people to be fast acting, and fast moving in the marketplace. We've got great leaders, and we continue to attract and promote great new leaders.

—Steve Ballmer

Innovation distinguishes between a leader and a follower.

—Steve Jobs

A great leader is someone who practices what they preach. They lead by example, create a sense of loyalty and teamwork, and are active in the community sharing their success with those in need.

—Dave Thomas

In motivating people, you've got to engage their minds and their hearts. I motivate people, I hope, by example—and perhaps by excitement, by having productive ideas to make others feel involved.

—Rupert Murdoch

The most important thing I've learned since becoming CEO is context. It's how your company fits in with the world and how you respond to it.

—Jeff Immelt

Get me inside any boardroom and I'll get any decision I want.

—Alan Bond

Many great ideas go unexecuted, and many great executioners are without ideas. One without the other is worthless.

—Tim Blixseth

The growth and development of people is the highest calling of leadership.

—Harvey S. Firestone

It's more important to know your weaknesses than your strengths.

—Ray Lee Hunt

A strong player, which has the sufficient critical mass, can withhold pressure better and create a more stable environment that benefits shareholders as well as employees.

—Lakshmi Mittal

The worst disease which can afflict business executives in their work is not, as popularly supposed, alcoholism; it's egotism.

—Harold S. Geneen

I've never run into a guy who could win at the top level in anything today and didn't have the right attitude, didn't give it everything he had, at least while he was doing it; wasn't prepared and didn't have the whole program worked out.

—Ted Turner

But maybe because the dot-com world gives people positions at a younger age, and many women are prominent in this business, it will help change the view about who can run big companies.

—Christie Hefner

Far too many executives have become more concerned with the "four Ps"—pay, perks, power, and prestige—rather than making profits for shareholders.

—Scott McNealy

I am brave, but I take a view. It is an educated view.
I am careful. I am not reckless.

—Sir Philip Green

The easiest thing to find on God's green earth is someone to tell you all the things you cannot do.

—Richard M. DeVos

The American system of management, in my opinion, relies too much on outsiders to help make business decisions, and this is because of the insecurity that American decision makers feel in their jobs, as compared with most top Japanese corporate executives.

—Akio Morita

Once the rules are set, I would know which one would give me a better deal, . . . But you also run the danger the partner you want to choose would not be a successful partner. So preferably, if you can, partner with three, four or five of them, or the whole lot. One of them will get it!

—Kwek Leng Beng

You can be discouraged by failure or you can learn from it. So go ahead and make mistakes. Make all you can. Because remember, that's where you'll find success. On the far side.

—Thomas Watson

There are no crown princes at Ford.

—Edsel Ford

You don't want to get the same kind of advice from everyone on your board.

—Robert Cardenas

Being a CEO still means sitting across the table from big institutional investors and showing your leadership and having them believe in you.

—Christie Hefner

The quality of a leader is reflected in the standards they set for themselves.

—Ray Kroc

I never knock the opposition.

—John Anderson

You can know a person by the kind of desk he keeps. If the president of a company has a clean desk then it must be the executive vice president who is doing all the work.

—Harold S. Geneen

Everyone experiences tough times, it is a measure of your determination and dedication how you deal with them and how you can come through them.

—Lakshmi Mittal

I believe trust to be the essence of the ability to unify, to direct and to motivate, the three cardinal qualities of leadership. There are others: mental toughness, judgement, conviction, patience, enthusiasm—you could all add to this list—each quality taking precedence from the task to be done.

—Issy Sharp

Don't be afraid to make a mistake, your readers might like it.

—William Handolph Hearst

When your values are clear to you, making decisions becomes easier.

—Roy Disney

Nobody's irreplaceable, including me. I think for too long we've had a cult of personality in this company and in this industry, and frankly, I'd like to see that diminish.

—Bill Ford, Jr.

There are more pompous, arrogant, self-centered mediocre people running corporate America. Their judgments and misjudgments have made me rich.

—Joseph D. Jamail, Jr.

You can't run a business, or anything else, on a theory.

—Harold S. Geneen

Whatever we do has to be as good as any in the world.

—Irwin L. Jacobs

To succeed in business, to reach the top, an individual must know all it is possible to know about that business.

—J. Paul Getty

To hold others responsible for failure is a way of escaping one's own responsibility. Responsibility is a heavy burden and a great honour at the same time. Whoever shoulders responsibility must be worthy of it.

—Mohammad bin Rashid Al Maktoum

1,000,000,000
FEDERAL RESERVE NOTE
FF 95594731 A
F6
THE UNITED STATES OF AMERICA
THIS NOTE IS LEGAL TENDER FOR ALL DEBTS, PUBLIC AND PRIVATE
SERIES 2003 A
ONE BILLION DOLLARS
DALI
MADOFF

6

Investing

Don't gamble; take all your savings and buy some good stock and hold it till it goes up, then sell it. If it don't go up, don't buy it.

—Will Rogers

If you are ready and able to give up everything else—to study the whole history and background of the market and all of the principal companies whose stocks are on the board as carefully as a medical student studies anatomy, to glue your nose to the tape at the opening of every day of the year and never take it off until night—if you can do all that, and, in addition, you have the cool nerves of a great gambler, the sixth sense of a kind of clairvoyant, and the courage of a lion, you have a Chinaman's chance.

—Bernard Baruch

Finance is the art of passing money from hand to hand until it finally disappears.

—Robert W. Sarnoff

The way to make money is to buy when blood is running in the streets.

—John D. Rockefeller

Bulls make money. Bears make money. Pigs get slaughtered.

—source unknown

There are one hundred men seeking security to one able man who is willing to risk his fortune.

—J. Paul Getty

Investors have very short memories.

—Roman Abramovich

Wide diversification is only required when investors do not understand what they are doing.

—Warren Buffett

I buy when other people are selling.

—J. Paul Getty

At the time we acquired Viacom, everyone said I had overpaid. But even at today's depressed prices, that investment is worth billions. Everyone was saying MTV was a fad. I knew better.

—Sumner Redstone

Stock market bubbles don't grow out of thin air. They have a solid basis in reality, but reality as distorted by a misconception.

—George Soros

All we're doing is passing our savings on to our client base.

—Bernard Madoff, on electronic trading

Don't try to buy at the bottom and sell at the top. It can't be done except by liars.

—Bernard Baruch

October. This is one of the peculiarly dangerous months to speculate in stocks in. The others are July, January, September, April, November, May, March, June, December, August, and February.

—Mark Twain

The biggest mistake that I see people of wealth making is having a single-minded focus on investment returns with no thought about their spending patterns. At the end of the day, expense control plays a larger role in the success of a financial program than the entire array of specific investments.

—A. Michael Lipper

You've got to understand that markets go both ways, up and down. Over longer periods, stocks generally have always gone up. But any specific stock may never come back.

—Charles Schwab

If you have something at risk, you think differently.

—Henry Kravis

It's not the bulls and bears you need to avoid—it's the bum steers.

—Chuck Hills

I hate weekends because there is no stock market.

—Rene Rivkin

Chief executives, who themselves own few shares of their companies, have no more feeling for the average stockholder than they do for baboons in Africa.

—T. Boone Pickens

When good news about the market hits the front page of the *New York Times*, sell.

—Bernard Baruch

Markets are constantly in a state of uncertainty and flux and money is made by discounting the obvious and betting on the unexpected.

—George Soros

Do you know the only thing that gives me pleasure? It's to see my dividends coming in.

—John D. Rockefeller

The only shareholders who benefit are the ones who sell out, and who gives a damn for the shareholders who sell, . . . I care about the shareholders who are, not the shareholders who were.

—Peter Lewis

Invest in the business you know, not the business you hope to know.

—Melvin T. Reid

Why not invest your assets in the companies you really like? As Mae West said, "Too much of a good thing can be wonderful."

—Warren Buffett

When buying shares, ask yourself, would you buy the whole company?

—Rene Rivkin

Be careful what financial advice you listen to. Most financial advice—such as "save money," "get out of debt," "invest for the long term," and "diversify"—is fine for the middle class or the poor. It's not good advice if you want to be rich because it is obsolete advice.

—Robert Kiyosaki

A speculator is a man who observes the future and acts before it occurs.

—Bernard Baruch

Control of a company does not carry with it the ability to control the price of its stock.

—J. Paul Getty

Investments are like trains, and if you miss one, don't worry because another one will come down the line.

—Gerald W. Schwartz

Understanding how to be a good investor makes you a better business manager and vice versa.

—Charles Munger

My wheels are running. My investments are local, regional, and international.

—Prince Alwaleed Bin Talal Alsaud

I get afraid when everyone gets greedy;
but when everyone gets afraid, I get greedy.

—Warren Buffett

The financial markets generally are unpredictable. So that one has to have different scenarios . . . The idea that you can actually predict what's going to happen contradicts my way of looking at the market.

—George Soros

The main purpose of the stock market is to make fools of as many men as possible. If a speculator is correct half of the time, he is hitting a good average. Even being right three or four times out of ten should yield a person a fortune if he has the sense to cut his losses quickly on the ventures where he is wrong.

—Bernard Baruch

Only buy something that you'd be perfectly happy to hold if the market shut down for ten years.

—Warren Buffett

Buy an individual stock and you never know. You could go to zero.

—Charles Schwab

When beggars and shoeshine boys, barbers and beauticians can tell you how to get rich it is time to remind yourself that there is no more dangerous illusion than the belief that one can get something for nothing.

—Bernard Baruch

Every few seconds it changes—up an eighth, down an eighth—it's like playing a slot machine. I lose $20 million, I gain $20 million.

—Ted Turner

Bears don't live on Park Avenue.

—Bernard Baruch

The last thing you want to do, unless it's a very unusual situation, is to invest money.

—John Kluge

Italy is now a great country to invest in . . . today we have fewer communists and those who are still there deny having been one. Another reason to invest in Italy is that we have beautiful secretaries . . . superb girls.

—Silvio Berlusconi

I made my money by selling too soon.

—Bernard Baruch

It's one of the most important things at the end of the day, being able to say no to an investment.

—Henry Kravis

Buy when everyone else is selling and hold until everyone else is buying. That's not just a catchy slogan. It's the very essence of successful investing.

—J. Paul Getty

Never invest your money in anything that eats or needs repainting.

—Billy Rose

An investor is someone who knows some of the worst mistakes that can be made in business, and how to avoid them.

—Melvin T. Reid

Never pay the slightest attention to what a company president ever says about his stock.

—Bernard Baruch

Our favorite holding period is forever.

—Warren Buffett

Never follow the crowd.

—Bernard Baruch

In today's regulatory environment, it's virtually impossible to violate rules . . . but it's impossible for a violation to go undetected, certainly not for a considerable period of time.

—Bernard Madoff

7

Employees and Associates

I can't afford to pay them any other way.

—Andrew Carnegie, when asked how he can afford to pay his employees so well

Any man who does not carry with him the value of all of the men around him does not carry the value to spend my time.

—J. P. Morgan

Mr. Morgan buys his partners; I grow my own.

—Andrew Carnegie, on J. P. Morgan's practice of hiring associates who had already proved themselves elsewhere

Practice Golden-Rule 1 of Management in everything you do. Manage others the way you would like to be managed.

—Brian Tracy

I always like to refer managers in corporate America as the renters of the corporate assets, not the owners.

—Henry Kravis

A committee is a cul-de-sac down which ideas are lured and then quietly strangled.

—Sir Barnett Cocks

If you pay peanuts, you get monkeys.

—Sir James Goldsmith

I surrounded myself with a lot of talent—legal talent, financial talent—to make sure that everything we did, was and looked and smelled proper and correct.

—Ronald Perelman

I always felt that our people came first. Some of the business schools regarded that as a conundrum. They would say: Which comes first, your people, your customers, or your shareholders? And I would say, it's not a conundrum. Your people come first, and if you treat them right, they'll treat the customers right, and the customers will come back, and that'll make the shareholders happy.

—Herb Kelleher

I think my most important job in IBM is working with anybody who has a problem.

—Thomas Watson, Jr.

Working with great people who make it happen, and seeing the results.

—Wayne Huizenga, on the only thing that motivates him

Appreciate everything your associates do for the business. Nothing else can quite substitute for a few well-chosen, well-timed, sincere words of praise. They're absolutely free and worth a fortune.

—Sam Walton

In motivating people, you've got to engage their minds and their hearts. I motivate people, I hope, by example—and perhaps by excitement, by having productive ideas to make others feel involved.

—Rupert Murdoch

If you have lower than a 10 percent turnover, there is a problem. And if you have higher than, say 20 percent, there is a problem.

—William McGovern

I want people who will stand up to me. People who are not afraid to say exactly what's on their minds, even though that's probably not what I want to hear. That's what I want.

—Henry Kravis

I think you have to work with people, and when I talk about managing relationships, don't think the derogatory "managed relationships." It is a question of sharing emotion and feelings. The common denominator of everything can't be money, and it should not be money.

—Anil Ambani

Play off everyone against each other so that you have more avenues of action open to you.

—Howard Hughes

Whenever there is a hard job to be done I assign it to a lazy man; he is sure to find an easy way of doing it.

—Walter Chrysler

I have no use for men who fail. The cause of their failure is no business of mine, but I want successful men as my associates.

—John D. Rockefeller

These great guys who ran corporate businesses in New York . . . they'd ask me what our greatest competitive advantage was with Kinko's, and I said it was a spark in our workers' eyes. And they didn't realize that.

—Paul Orfalea

I don't pay good wages because I have a lot of money; I have a lot of money because I pay good wages.

—Robert Bosch

The people in the middle are my employees, and if they're not aligned to those customers, then it is my job to make them aligned. A lot of times middle managers take their eyes off the ball, which is to take care of their customers and workers.

—Paul Orfalea

Our "People, Service, Profit" philosophy insists that our people be treated fairly. If we give good service and we come up with a reasonable profit, we make that a good deal for our employees, with profit sharing, promotions, complaint procedures.

—Frederick W. Smith

The employer generally gets the employees he deserves.

—J. Paul Getty

In all my years in business I can recall very few people I have wanted to fire for making mistakes.

—Akio Morita

Good personnel will work for a competent manager. Go to every length to find, hire, and train good employees and treat them like your family. This is the crux of your whole operation.

—J. Willard Marriott

Appreciate everything your associates do for the business. If people believe in themselves, it's amazing what they can accomplish.

—Sam Walton

If warehouse managers know that their own regional bosses have open door policies and will talk to any employees about their issues, then they are going to be a little faster to talk to the troubled employees themselves. They don't want the problems to come back to them through their bosses.

—Jim Sinegal

Compromise is usually bad. It should be a last resort. If two departments or divisions have a problem they can't solve and it comes up to you, listen to both sides and then pick one or the other. This places solid accountability on the winner to make it work. Condition your people to avoid compromise.

—Robert Townsend

First of all, if you come here, you'll be happy. And No. 2, if you come here, you'll be the most highly compensated employee in the airline industry. Not compensated the way other airlines compensate people, but when you put it all together, why do you care?

—Herb Kelleher

The five steps in teaching an employee new skills are preparation, explanation, showing, observation and supervision.

—Harold Hook

If you can't finish this job today, maybe I can't sign your check on payday.

—John Johnson

I established the rule that once we hire an employee, his schools records are a matter of the past, and are no longer used to evaluate his work or decide on his promotion.

—Akio Morita

We don't have as many managers as we should, but we would rather have too few than too many.

—Larry Page

I make more money than my competition who pays 50 cents an hour because of the efficiencies of dealing with someone face to face and paying them a fair wage.

—Dov Charney

If the frontline people do count, you couldn't prove it by examining the reward systems in most organizations.

—Karl Albrecht

If you don't know what to do with many of the papers piled on your desk, stick a dozen colleagues' initials on them and pass them along. When in doubt, route.

—Malcolm S. Forbes

If we hire people who are smaller than we are, we will become a company of dwarfs. If we hire people who are larger than we are, we'll become a company of giants.

—David Ogilvy

Businesses are all relationships, based on common values, values such as staying true to your word. Every religion also enshrines those values, so you can have different religious beliefs, but underlying those beliefs, you've got people who must have similar values, and can work together.

—Issy Sharp

Failure to delegate is the biggest single obstacle to job performance in IBM.

—Thomas Watson, Jr.

Our company is built on people—those who work for us, and those we do business with.

—Harvey S. Firestone

I would rather earn 1% off 100 people's efforts than 100% of my own efforts.

—John D. Rockefeller

One of the hallmarks of Onex is that since I started the company in 1983, every professional who has joined the company at our Toronto head office is still here. We've had no turnover.

—Gerald W. Schwartz

Anytime you're in a pressure situation, you find out who's going to step up and do it and who's going to fade into the background.

—Eric Schmidt

When you hire people that are smarter than you are, you prove you are smarter than they are.

—R. H. Grant

Be nice to nerds. Chances are you'll end up working for one.

—Bill Gates

A man is known by the company he keeps. A company is known by the men it keeps.

—Thomas Watson

If you want to give a man credit, put it in writing.
If you want to give him hell, do it on the phone.

—Charles Beecham

I was once an employee myself, so I know what employees want.

—Li Ka-shing

It's not necessary to be so structured in this world. With all the people who work here, whether you are real structured or not, it is not going to affect how much work they do. People have inside of them a certain work ethic, and, if you appeal to them nicely, they'll respond and give all they can give.

—Fred DeLuca

We have a culture that allows us to change without threatening the people that work at the company.

—Frederick W. Smith

It was my philosophy to treat the franchise owners as partners.

—Ron Joyce

When you are dealing with employees, you are dealing with a total person—the whole enchilada of the worker. A worker might have a problem with her husband, but you've still got to get a smile on her face. That's your problem. When workers have mood problems because they've got baggage, that's your problem.

—Paul Orfalea

We hire on requirement basis and not on anticipation.

—Azim Premji

There is an old saying that when you talk—you teach, when you listen—you learn. There are a lot of ideas worth listening to in this company. Let's be sure we're paying attention. We are never so rich in ideas that we can afford not to.

—Thomas Watson, Jr.

You never really hear the truth from your subordinates until after ten in the evening.

—Jurgen Schrempp

To succeed as a team is to hold all of the members accountable for their expertise.

—Mitchell Caplan

Sandwich every bit of criticism between two thick layers of praise.

—Mary Kay Ash

We will ensure that associates continue to possess unsurpassed product knowledge and maintain their dedication to customer service and respect for their colleagues and for the communities in which they work and live.

—Arthur Blank

It doesn't matter to me if a man is from Harvard or Sing Sing. We hire the man, not his history.

—Henry Ford

Diversity: the art of thinking independently together.

—Malcolm S. Forbes

The ability to deal with people is as purchasable a commodity as sugar or coffee and I will pay more for that ability than for any other under the sun.

—John D. Rockefeller

A businessman once said, "A business succeeds not because it is long established or because it is big, but because there are men and women in it who live it, sleep it, dream it, and build great future plans for it."

—J. Willard Marriott

I love the ability to work with very good managers, and to provide the right incentives for them, and truly become a partner with that management, and make that management take a long view.

—Henry Kravis

I've heard that some coaches face a curious dilemma. The world-class athletes on their teams—the players with the best skills and experience—sometimes falter when it comes to crunch time. Occasionally, though, there's a player on the team, a blue-collar guy whose skills and training are not quite world-class. Yet at crunch time, he's the one the coach sends out to the field. He's so driven and so hungry to win that he can outperform the top athletes when it really matters.

—Howard Schultz

One of the managers in our People Department once said, "The important thing is to take the bricklayer and make him understand that he's building a home, not just laying bricks." So we take the building-a-home approach: This is what you're doing not only for yourself but for society: giving people who'd otherwise not be able to travel the opportunity to do so.

—Herb Kelleher

I can walk through the front door of any factory and out the back and tell you if it's making money or not. I can just tell by the way it's being run and by the spirit of the workers.

—Harvey S. Firestone

I make progress by having people around me who are smarter than I am and listening to them. And I assume that everyone is smarter about something than I am.

—Henry J. Kaiser

I've got America's best writer for $300 a week.

—Jack L. Warner

People are definitely a company's greatest asset. It doesn't make any difference whether the product is cars or cosmetics. A company is only as good as the people it keeps.

—Mary Kay Ash

Somehow, despite the greatest differences in temperaments and even in interests, somehow we had to work together. We were an organization. At the center of our lives—our job, our function—at that point everything we had belonged to each other.

—Henry R. Luce

To be at the top we get service standards down to the bottom of the pyramid, and that process begins for us with our hiring policy. We hire for attitude. We want people who like other people and are, therefore, more motivated to serve them. Competence we can teach. Attitude is ingrained.

—Issy Sharp

I figure that my staff will be less reluctant to work overtime if I work longer hours than they do.

—David Ogilvy

If you don't understand it, how do you expect me to understand it?

—John Johnson

You know the face of your worker . . . engineers and designers and finance people and knitters and dyers and chemists can come together in one location and say, "How can we do this better?" You can produce products more efficiently than they can be made on an outsource basis.

—Dov Charney

The golden rule of Domino's: Treat people as you want to be treated. I don't believe that in 38 years that I treated anyone unfairly. That may not be true, but as far as I know it is.

—Tom Monaghan

It's better to get smart than to get mad. I try not to get so insulted that I will not take advantage of an opportunity to persuade people to change their minds.

—John Johnson

We have a good many MBAs, but we look at them for attitude as well. We will hire someone with less experience, less education, and less expertise, than someone who has more of those things and has a rotten attitude. Because we can train people. We can teach people how to lead. We can teach people how to provide customer service. But we can't change their DNA.

—Herb Kelleher

I'm looking for people who are bright, have the highest ethical standards, will not compromise one iota for that.

—Henry Kravis

A customer is the most important person ever in this office—in person or by mail.

—Leon Leonwood Bean

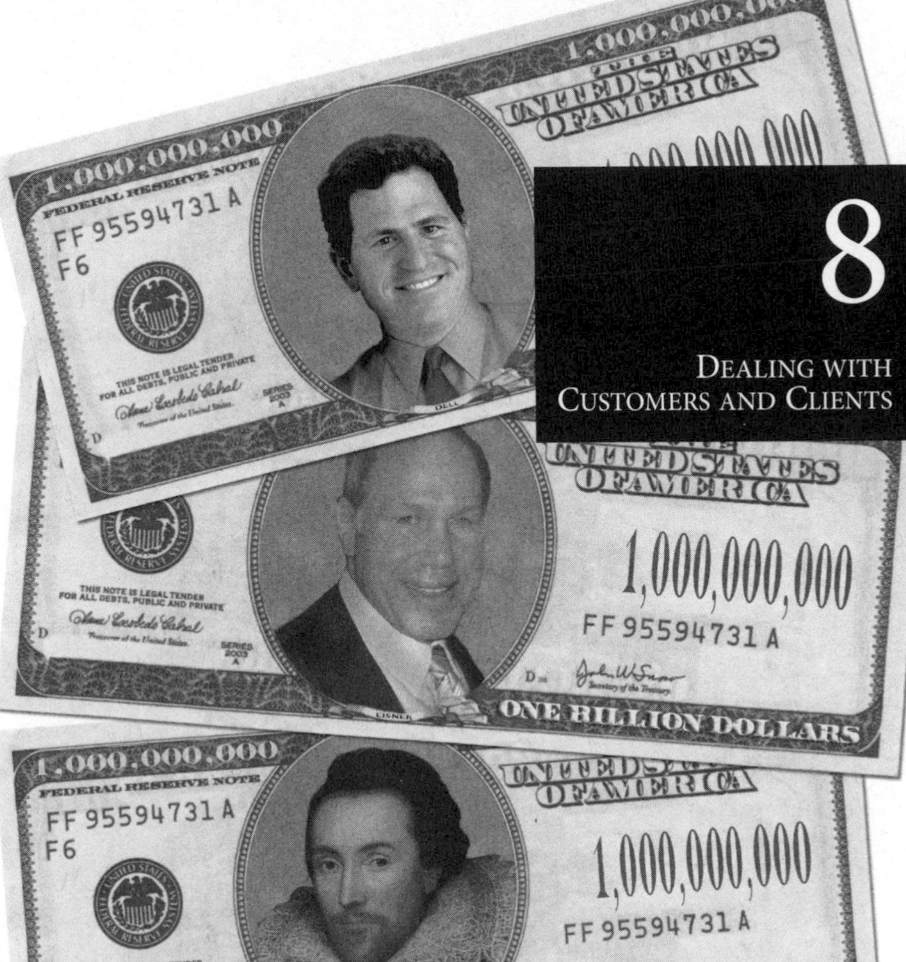

8

Dealing with Customers and Clients

The customer is always right.

—attributed to Marshall Field

It is not the employer who pays the wages. Employers only handle the money. It is the customer who pays the wages.

—Henry Ford

Politeness and civility are the best capital ever invested in business. Large stores, gilt signs, flaming advertisements, will all prove unavailing if you or your employees treat your patrons abruptly.

—Phineas T. Barnum

We consider our customers a part of our organization, and we want them to feel free to make any criticism they see fit in regard to our merchandise or service.

—Leon Leonwood Bean

If you don't care, your customer never will.

—Marlene Blaszczyk

Treat your customers like lifetime partners.

—Michael LeBoeuf

If you're not serving the customer, you'd better be serving someone who is.

—Karl Albrecht

Your most unhappy customers are your greatest source of learning.

—Bill Gates

Our vision and our mandate is to give customers the kind of holistic, simple experiences they want, and we do that every day.

—Steve Ballmer

What pays under capitalism is satisfying the common man, the customer. The more people you satisfy, the better for you.

—Ludwig von Mises

In the end, the customer doesn't know, or care, if you are small or large as an organization . . . she or he only focuses on the garment hanging on the rail in the store.

—Giorgio Armani

If you do build a great experience, customers tell each other about that. Word of mouth is very powerful.

—Jeff Bezos

Some people find an interest in making money, and though they appear to be slaving, many actually enjoy every minute of their work.

—Walter Annenberg

Good will is the one and only asset that competition cannot undersell or destroy.

—Marshall Field

I am the world's worst salesman, therefore,
I must make it easy for people to buy.

—F. W. Woolworth

I think that more companies are now realizing its corporate reputation is at stake and what they fear mostly is consumer revolt.

—Anita Roddick

Above all, we wish to avoid having a dissatisfied customer.

—Leon Leonwood Bean

[The customers are] defining the experience, not us. We're just letting it rip. What I'm basically trying to say is that as long as we don't screw it up, we'll be fine.

—Tom Anderson and Chris De Wolfe

The people in the front lines are my customers. I need to keep them happy. And, the best way to take care of your customers is to take care of your workers.

—Paul Orfalea

There is only one boss: the customer. And he can fire everybody in the company, from the chairman on down, simply by spending his money somewhere else.

—Sam Walton

Our planning system was dynamite when we first put it in. The thinking was fresh; the form mattered little. It was idea oriented. We then hired a head of planning, and he hired two vice presidents, and then he hired a planner; and the books got thicker, and the printing more sophisticated, and the covers got harder, and the drawings got better.

—John Welch

With businesses, you go to the same places because you like the service, you like the people and they take care of you. They greet you with a smile. That's how people want to be treated, with respect. That's what I tell my employees—customer service is very important.

—Ervin "Magic" Johnson

To me what mattered most was never to register more sales in the cash register. The only thing that mattered to me was to register a smile on a customer's face. If you can get a customer to smile, we will succeed.

—Debbi Fields

If you're able to listen to customers from their perspective, not everything they say will make sense. Not everything they do will be right. But you'll know more about what you have to do because of it.

—Peter van Stolk

I founded the company on the notion that people were basically good and that if you give them the benefit of the doubt you're rarely disappointed.

—Pierre Omidyar

When you stop talking, you've lost your customer.
When you turn your back, you've lost her.

—Estee Lauder

The definition of salesmanship is the gentle art of letting the customer have it your way.

—Ray Kroc

We can believe that we know where the world should go. But unless we're in touch with our customers, our model of the world can diverge from reality. There's no substitute for innovation, of course, but innovation is no substitute for being in touch, either.

—Steve Ballmer

Take care of your customers and employees first, and profits will follow.

—Jack C. Taylor

Users told us what they wanted to see, and we just built it. That's how we do a lot of our updates. We catalog what people tell us that they want. It's not super-complicated.

—Tom Anderson and Chris De Wolfe

We see our customers as invited guests to a party, and we are the hosts. It's our job every day to make every important aspect of the customer experience a little bit better.

—Jeff Bezos

Criticism doesn't bother me. What we've tried to do inside FedEx is to say that criticism is a real opportunity to improve. When we do something wrong for a customer, that's when we really have a chance to learn how to do things better.

—Frederick W. Smith

You need to first understand what their [the customers'] needs are. You have to empathize and understand what their problems are. You might not be able to solve everybody's problems, but you have to at least be able to understand them.

—Paul Orfalea

We were resolute to do what our users wanted. Having discipline and saying no is why we ended up being so successful.

—Tom Anderson and Chris De Wolfe

Sell good merchandise at a reasonable profit, treat your customers like human beings, and they will always come back for more.

—Leon Leonwood Bean

Carefully watch how people live, get an intuitive sense as to what they might want and then go with it. Don't do market research.

—Akio Morita

The nature of any human being, certainly anyone on Wall Street, is "the better deal you give the customer, the worse deal it is for you."

—Bernard Madoff

1,000,000,000
FEDERAL RESERVE NOTE
FF 95594731 A
F6
THE UNITED STATES OF AMERICA
1,000,000,000
FF 95594731 A
ONE BILLION DOLLARS

9

Proverbially Rich

With money, you can make the devil push a millstone.

—Chinese proverb

Get what you can and keep what you have; that's the way to get rich.

—Scottish proverb

It's not money that brings happiness, it's lots of money.

—Russian proverb

With money you're a dragon; without it you're a worm.

—Chinese proverb

A wealthy man always has followers.

—proverb that appears in several cultures

Money earned with pains should be spent on pleasure.

—Chinese proverb

No one is poor but he thinks himself so.

—Portuguese proverb

'Tis money that begets money.

—English proverb

Money makes money, and the money that money makes makes more money.

—Italian proverb (and the theory of compund interest)

Money can move the gods.

—Chinese proverb

With money in your pocket, you are wise and you are handsome and you sing well too.

—Yiddish proverb

Only after the last tree has been cut down, Only after the last river has been poisoned, Only after the last fish has been caught, Only then will you find that money cannot be eaten.

—Cree Indian prophecy

Poverty is no disgrace, but it's also no great honour.

—Yiddish proverb

When the sea turned into honey, the beggar lost his spoon.

—Bulgarian proverb

Penny wise and pound foolish.

—Scottish proverb

A rich man has more relations than he knows.

—French proverb

A fool may earn money, but it takes a wise man to keep it.

—Scottish proverb

If you cannot become rich, be the neighbour of a rich man.

—Armenian proverb

A heart free from care is better than a full purse.

—Arab proverb

He who has money can eat ice cream in hell.

—Lebanese proverb

Too much prosperity makes most men fools.

—Italian proverb

Money is only good for a weekday, a holiday, and a rainy day.

—Russian proverb

If the rich could hire others to die for them, the poor could make a nice living.

—Yiddish proverb

Those who have money go abroad in the world, but those who have no suitable clothes are reluctant to do so.

—Chinese proverb

Great riches come from heaven; small riches come from diligence.

—Chinese proverb

Cut your losses and let your profits run.

—American proverb

Business is like a wheelbarrow—it stands still until someone pushes it.

—American proverb

A wealthy man always has followers.

—Proverb found in many cultures

If thou art poor, do not make a rich man thy friend.

—Arab proverb

Money makes people brash; if they do not speak well, they just shout.

—Chinese proverb

If thou goest to a foreign country, do not alight at a rich man's house.

—Arab proverb

It is better to be poor and live long than rich and die young.

—proverb found in many cultures

10

Other Thoughts

Nowadays, anyone who cannot speak English and is incapable of using the Internet is regarded as backward.

—Prince Alwaleed Bin Talal Alsaud

If the spirit of business adventure is dulled, this country will cease to hold the foremost position in the world.

—Andrew Mellon

The future may be made up of many factors but where it truly lies is in the hearts and minds of men. Your dedication should not be confined for your own gain, but unleashes your passion for our beloved country as well as for the integrity and humanity of mankind.

—Li Ka-shing

You will not be satisfied unless you are contributing something to or for the benefit of others.

—Walter Annenberg

Golf courses are the best place to observe ministers, but none of them are above cheating a bit.

—John D. Rockefeller

With some exceptions, the wrong people are running U.S. companies. It's been that way for years, and it hasn't gotten much better.

—Carl Icahn

You have undertaken to cheat me.
I won't sue you, for the law is too slow. I will ruin you.
—Cornelius Vanderbilt

In general, the art of government consists in taking as much money as possible from one party of the citizens to give to the other.

—François-Marie Voltaire

Making mistakes is the privilege of the active. It is always the mediocre people who are negative, who spend their time proving that they were not wrong.

—Ingvar Kamprad

My view is to give everyone the space to grow in his own way. When you see restructuring or separations in a family [firm], value has almost always been destroyed. This is the first case where value has been enhanced. In that way it has been a win-win ending.

—Mukesh Ambani

If you deeply appreciate and love what creative people do and how they think, which is usually in unpredictable and irrational ways, then you can start to understand them. And finally, you can see inside their minds and DNA.

—Bernard Arnault

Today I see a billion people as a billion potential consumers, an opportunity to generate value for them and to make a return for myself.

—Mukesh Ambani

Like almost everyone who uses e-mail, I receive a ton of spam every day. Much of it offers to help me get out of debt or get rich quick. It would be funny if it weren't so exciting.

—Bill Gates

I need to make an okay living. The people who work for us need to. But after you make a comfortable living, how much more do you need? It's like I make a joke about nerd values, because I'm very much in the rich nerd tradition. And you know, we say, like, hey, people pay us for this stuff, like programming. You know, what else do we need?

—Craig Newmark

My parents shared not only an improbable love, they shared an abiding faith in the possibilities of this nation. They would give me an African name, Barack, or blessed, believing that in a tolerant America your name is no barrier to success. They imagined me going to the best schools in the land, even though they weren't rich, because in a generous America you don't have to be rich to achieve your potential.

—Barack Obama

For all of its faults, [capitalism] gives most hardworking people a chance to improve themselves economically, even as the deck is stacked in favor of the privileged few. Here are the choices most of us face in such a system: Get bitter or get busy.

—Bill O'Reilly

I think one can achieve a very pleasant lifestyle by treating human beings, fellow human beings, very well . . .

—Rene Rivkin

All programming for prosperity should be built on spiritual foundations. The first step is to enter the spiritual dimension, the alpha level, and determine what your purpose in life is. Find out what you are here for, what you are supposed to do with your life.

—Jose Silva

Everybody today seems to be in such a terrible rush, anxious for greater developments and greater riches and so on, so that children have very little time for their parents. Parents have very little time for each other, and in the home begins the disruption of peace of the world.

—Mother Teresa

I remain very much connected to my childhood . . . I have never been too jaded or too sophisticated—it keeps me alive every day.

—Hugh Hefner

To succeed, you will soon learn, as I did, the importance of a solid foundation in the basics of education—literacy, both verbal and numerical, and communication skills.

—Alan Greenspan

If you don't have integrity, you have nothing. You can't buy it. You can have all the money in the world, but if you are not a moral and ethical person, you really have nothing.

—Henry Kravis

It boils down to luck. Circumstances could have been otherwise.

—Ernest Gallo

Luck is a dividend of sweat. The more you sweat, the luckier you get.

—Ray Kroc

What I try to do as I'm going up the trail, I try to bring with me other African-Americans who can then use my experience and gain credibility from what I've done to be their own successful person.

—Robert Johnson

What we do during our working hours determines what we have; what we do in our leisure hours determines what we are.

—George Eastman

Life's like a movie, write your own ending.
Keep believing, keep pretending.

—Jim Henson

I like to think in terms of giving people an understanding of why they should have the same passion as I do—why their life has purpose working here and why they should believe as much as I believe. I want them to seek a higher level of satisfaction above just making a salary.

—Charles Schwab

Life is too complicated not to be orderly.

—Martha Stewart

Today the strategies of many companies in the real estate industry are premised on low interest rates, an assumption that has resulted in the rapid expansion of the real estate securitization business. This trend could be regarded as a risk factor, as it exposes the real estate sector to at least three potential problems: first, interest rate hikes; second, revisions to securitization business accounting standards; and third, overheating in the real estate market.

—Akira Mori

I know that I have the ability to achieve the object of my Definite Purpose in life, therefore, I demand of myself persistent, continuous action toward its attainment, and I here and now promise to render such action.

—Napoleon Hill

Climate change poses clear, catastrophic threats. We may not agree on the extent, but we certainly can't afford the risk of inaction.

—Rupert Murdoch

The United States has got some of the dumbest people in the world. I want you to know that we know that.

—Ted Turner

In life and business, there are two cardinal sins . . . The first is to act precipitously without thought and the second is to not act at all.

—Carl Icahn

People are surprised to find out that an awful lot of people think that they're idiots.

—Eric Schmidt

I did something that challenged the banking world. Conventional banks look for the rich; we look for the absolutely poor. All people are entrepreneurs, but many don't have the opportunity to find that out.

—Muhammad Yunus

The present era has no comparable referent in the past history of capitalism. We have a higher percentage of the intelligentsia engaged in buying and selling pieces of paper and promoting trading activity than in any past era. A lot of what I see now reminds me of Sodom and Gomorrah. You get activity feeding on itself, envy and imitation. It has happened in the past that there came bad consequences.

—Charles Munger

News is something somebody doesn't want printed; all else is advertising.

—William Handolph Hearst

You cannot spend money in luxury without doing good to the poor. Nay, you do more good to them by spending it in luxury, than by giving it; for by spending it in luxury, you make them exert industry, whereas by giving it, you keep them idle.

—Samuel Johnson

Actually I am very glad that people can buy Armani—even if it's a fake. I like the fact that I'm so popular around the world.

—Giorgio Armani

The real source of wealth and capital in this new era is not material things . . . it is the human mind, the human spirit, the human imagination, and our faith in the future.

—Steve Forbes

I think if you look at people, whether in business or government, who haven't had any moral compass, who've just changed to say whatever they thought the popular thing was, in the end they're losers.

—Michael Bloomberg

I am just a person who is human, down to earth enjoying life . . . whatever god blesses you with. Enjoying life for me is just normal.

—Mohamed Al-Fayed

This is a world in which reasons are made up because reality is too painful.

—Barry Diller

Vision is perhaps our greatest strength . . . it has kept us alive to the power and continuity of thought through the centuries, it makes us peer into the future and lends shape to the unknown.

—Li Ka-shing

A whale is harpooned only when it spouts.

—Henry Hillman

It's all about quality of life and finding a happy balance between work and friends and family.

—Sir Philip Green

Everybody has to be somebody to somebody to be anybody.

—Malcolm S. Forbes

I do not think that there is any other quality so essential to success of any kind as the quality of perseverance. It overcomes almost everything, even nature.

—John D. Rockefeller

Regrets and recriminations only hurt your soul.

—Armand Hammer

We must have a theme, a goal, a purpose in our lives. If you don't know where you're aiming, you don't have a goal. My goal is to live my life in such a way that when I die, someone can say, "She cared."

—Mary Kay Ash

There are two things needed in these days; first, for rich men to find out how poor men live; and second, for poor men to know how rich men work.

—Edward Atkinson

Of all the things that can have an effect on your future, I believe personal growth is the greatest. We can talk about sales growth, profit growth, asset growth, but all of this probably will not happen without personal growth.

—Jim Rohn

Should you find yourself in a chronically leaking boat, energy devoted to changing vessels is likely to be more productive than energy devoted to patching leaks.

—Warren Buffett

Diversity is a great force towards creativity.

—Michael Eisner

Any man who has the brains to think and the nerve to act for the benefit of the people of the country is considered a radical by those who are content with stagnation and willing to endure disaster.

—William Handolph Hearst

In times of rapid change, experience could be your worst enemy.

—J. Paul Getty

I see nothing . . . in the present situation that is either menacing or warrants pessimism. During the winter months there may be some slackness or unemployment but hardly more than at this season each year. I have every confidence that there will be a revival of activity in the spring, and that during the coming year the country will make steady progress.

—Treasury Secretary Andrew W. Mellon, December 31, 1929, in a statement issued while yachting off Nassau, the Bahamas, on his winter vacation

You should set goals beyond your reach
so you always have something to live for.

—Ted Turner

I believe that thrift is essential to well-ordered living.

—John D. Rockefeller

I believe that the rendering of useful service is the common duty of mankind and that only in the purifying fire of sacrifice is the dross of selfishness consumed and the greatness of the human soul set free.

—John D. Rockefeller, Jr.

Father [John D. Rockefeller, Jr.] was the eldest son and the heir apparent, and he set the standard for being a Rockefeller very high, so every achievement was taken for granted and perfection was the norm.

—David Rockefeller

Genius is 1% inspiration and 99% perspiration. Accordingly a genius is often merely a talented person who has done all of his or her homework.

—Thomas Edison

Ridiculous yachts and private planes and big limousines won't make people enjoy life more, and it sends out terrible messages to the people who work for them. It would be so much better if that money was spent in Africa—and it's about getting a balance.

—Richard Branson

One problem people have is that they lie to themselves. You may think you are more talented than the next guy. Which is exactly what the next guy thinks as well.

—Mark Cuban

A government cannot be expected to allow independence to its central bank unless that bank is also accountable to it and to the wider public. That is, the central bank must be able to be judged on whether or not it has achieved its agreed objective.

—Ian Macfarlane

The cynics will tell you that the good you do today will be forgotten tomorrow. Just do it anyway.

—Roberto C. Goizueta

You can't sit on the lid of progress. If you do, you will be blown to pieces.

—Henry J. Kaiser

All my life people have said that I wasn't going to make it.

—Ted Turner

The will to work of everyone in the country is the best guarantee of national survival.

—Bhumibol Adulyadej

I think if you look at people, whether in business or government, who haven't had any moral compass, who've just changed to say whatever they thought the popular thing was, in the end they're losers.

—Michael Bloomberg

Superstition is the poison of the mind.

—Joseph Lewis

My idea is always to avoid nostalgia.

—Miuccia Prada

Failure is simply the opportunity to begin again, this time more intelligently.

—Henry Ford

Family, religion, friends . . . these are the three demons you must slay if you wish to succeed in business.

—Charles Montgomery "Monty" Burns

As we go forward, I hope we're going to continue to use technology to make really big differences in how people live and work.

—Sergey Brin

The property boom has made us all feel wealthy, but unfortunately it has lulled many of those nearing retirement into a false sense of security.

—Noel Whittaker

A man should never neglect his family for business.

—Walt Disney

Don't spend time beating on a wall,
hoping to transform it into a door.

—Coco Chanel

A person who retires feeling that he has done his bit will quickly wither away.

—Ingvar Kamprad

I have no Napoleonic dream. I'm just hard-working and pragmatic.

—Roman Abramovich

I didn't go to high school, and I didn't go to grade school either. Education, I think, is for refinement and is probably a liability.

—H. L. Hunt

The role we can play every day, if we try, is to take the whole experience of every day and shape it to involve American man. It is our job to interest him in his community and to give his ideas the excitement they should have.

—John Hay Whitney

Diamonds are nothing more than chunks of coal that stuck to their jobs.

—Malcolm S. Forbes

We at Chrysler borrow money the old-fashioned way. We pay it back.

—Lee Iacocca

Often undecided whether to desert a sinking ship for one that might not float, he would make up his mind to sit on the wharf for a day.

—Lord Beaverbrook

God help us if we ever take the theater out of the auction business or anything else. It would be an awfully boring world.

—A. Alfred Taubman

If necessity is the mother of invention, discontent is the father of progress.

—David Rockefeller

The American public tunes in every night hoping to see two people screwing. Obviously, we can't give them that but let's always keep it in mind.

—Barry Diller

The most powerful element in advertising is the truth.

—William Bernbach

Show me someone without an ego,
and I'll show you a loser.

—Donald Trump

The most important thing is God's blessing and if you believe in God and you believe in yourself, you have nothing to worry about.

—Mohamed Al-Fayed

I think life is sort of like a competition, whether it's in sports, or it's achieving in school, or it's achieving good relationships with people. And competition is a little bit of what it's all about.

—Sanford I. Weill

A man with a surplus can control circumstances, but a man without a surplus is controlled by them, and often has no opportunity to exercise judgment.

—Harvey S. Firestone

No sale, no commission. No commission, no eat.
That made an impression on me.

—David Ogilvy

I have my own definition for the term "retirement." Life was extremely hard when I was young; today working without the burden of pressure to me is the same as the luxury of retirement.

—Li Ka-shing

Concentration can be cultivated. One can learn to exercise will power, discipline one's body and train one's mind.

—Anil Ambani

People first, then money, then things.

—Suze Orman

In retailing, the formula happens to be a basic liking for human beings, plus integrity, plus industry, plus the ability to see the other fellow's point of view.

—James Cash Penny

I thought I'd have assistants do that stuff for me, which is why I missed the value of the digital era in so many ways. You can't understand the power of technology unless you use it.

—Gerald W. Schwartz

Power corrupts. Absolute power is kind of neat.

—John F. Lehman, Jr.

The big will get bigger; the small will get wiped out.

—Charles Revson

In my own work, I've tried to anticipate what's coming over the horizon, to hasten its arrival, and to apply it to people's lives in a meaningful way.

—Paul Allen

The feeling of having finished something is an effective sleeping pill.

—Ingvar Kamprad

We are approaching a new age of synthesis. Knowledge cannot be merely a degree or a skill . . . it demands a broader vision, capabilities in critical thinking and logical deduction without which we cannot have constructive progress.

—Li Ka-shing

Taxes are not good things, but if you want services, somebody's got to pay for them so they're a necessary evil.

—Michael Bloomberg

All money nowadays seems to be produced with a natural homing instinct for the Treasury.

—Prince Philip, Duke of Edinburgh

I have no friends and no enemies—only competitors.

—Aristotle Onassis

There seems to be some perverse human characteristic that likes to make easy things difficult.

—Warren Buffett

An optimist feels these are the best of times; the pessimist feels the optimist may be right.

—Morton Zuckerman

Your mentors in life are important, so choose them wisely.

—Robert Kiyosaki

I have always believed that it's important to show a new look periodically. Predictability can lead to failure.

—T. Boone Pickens

The trouble in America is not that we are making too many mistakes, but that we are making too few.

—Philip Knight

I believe in the Scottish proverb: "Hard work never killed a man." Men die of boredom, psychological conflict, and disease. They do not die of hard work.

—David Ogilvy

Be careful to leave your sons well instructed rather than rich, for the hopes of the instructed are better than the wealth of the ignorant.

—Epictetus

To truly prepare for the unexpected, you've got to position yourself to keep a couple of options open so when the door of opportunity opens, you're close enough to squeeze through.

—Pierre Omidyar

You need to have a passionate interest in why things are happening. That cast of mind, kept over long periods, gradually improves your ability to focus on reality. If you don't have the cast of mind, you're destined for failure even if you have a high I.Q.

—Charles Munger

You can believe in Fung Shui if you want, but ultimately people control their own fate. The most important thing is to improve yourself and give it your best. Then many things previously thought to be impossible will become possible.

—Li Ka-shing

When a mature and able manager feels bored, he should seriously consider changing jobs, changing companies or simply retiring. It is not fair to anyone for half a leader to hold a full-time leadership job.

—James L. Hayes

Why pay a dollar for a bookmark? Why not use the dollar for a bookmark?

—Steven Spielberg

I supposed it would have been great to invent something as classic and enduring as the tuxedo. But if I was collecting royalties, I wish I'd invented the corkscrew.

—Giorgio Armani

I believe in nurturing creativity and offering a haven for creators, enabling them to develop their ideas to the fullest. With more and more talented creators being drawn to Cirque in an environment that fulfills them, these are ideal to continue developing great new shows.

—Guy Laliberte

We need to push ourselves to make as many reductions as possible in our own energy use first . . . and that takes time. But we must do this quickly . . . the climate will not wait for us.

—Rupert Murdoch

I find that when you have a real interest in life and a curious life, that sleep is not the most important thing.

—Martha Stewart

A nation is not in danger of financial disaster merely because it owes itself money.

—Andrew Mellon

The three great essentials to achieve anything worthwhile are, first, hard work; second, stick-to-itiveness; third, common sense.

—Thomas Edison

You can't succeed unless you've got failure, especially creatively.

—Michael Eisner

Creativity is a highfalutin word for the work I have to do between now and Tuesday.

—Ray Kroc

There's nothing wrong with being fired.

—Ted Turner

When everything seems to be going against you, remember that the airplane takes off against the wind, not with it.

—Henry Ford

A good person can make another person good; it means that goodness will elicit goodness in the society; other persons will also be good.

—Bhumibol Adulyadej

Take the pains required to become what you want to become, or you might end up becoming something you'd rather not be. That is also a daily discipline and worth considering.

—Donald Trump

Innovation! One cannot be forever innovating. I want to create classics.

—Coco Chanel

Here's what would be pitiful . . . if your income grew, but you didn't.

—Jim Rohn

In a perfect world, we'd all be judged on the sweetness of our souls. But in our less than perfect world, the woman who looks pretty has a distinct advantage and, usually, the last word.

—Estee Lauder

To be happy in this world, first you need a cell phone and then you need an airplane. Then you're truly wireless.

—Ted Turner

I want a lawyer to tell me what I cannot do. I hire him to tell how to do what I want to do.

—J. P. Morgan

The true measure of a career is to be able to be content, even proud, that you succeeded through your own endeavors without leaving a trail of casualties in your wake.

—Alan Greenspan

If you expect nothing, you're apt to be surprised. You'll get it.

—Malcolm S. Forbes

Don't be threatened by people smarter than you. Compromise anything but your core values. Seek to renew yourself even when you are hitting home runs. And everything matters.

—Howard Schultz

I am convinced that, under the threat of the impoverishment of our people, the machinery of government must be simplified to the utmost.

—Gustav Krupp

To be fair is not enough any more. We must be ferociously fair.

—John Hay Whitney

I have learned to enjoy the ups for what they are, because those are the moments that feel like they go by the quickest.

—Sean "P. Diddy" Combs

I thought, you know, you have so many positives in your life, you have a wonderful family, you have good health, you have had wonderful success in business, why focus on the one negative thing? So I just kind of gave myself a talking to and said look, you know, get this thing done. You can do it.

—Jenny Craig

I made a resolve then that I was going to amount to something if I could. And no hours, nor amount of labour, nor amount of money would deter me from giving the best that there was in me. And I have done that ever since, and I win by it. I know.

—Colonel Harlan Sanders

Good enough never is. Set your standards so high that even the flaws are considered excellent.

—Debbi Fields

The music industry is a strange combination of having real and intangible assets: pop bands are brand names in themselves, and at a given stage in their careers their name alone can practically guarantee hit records.

—Richard Branson

The difference between style and fashion is quality.

—Giorgio Armani

Whatever you tax, you get less of.

—Alan Greenspan

You walk very slowly and maybe by chance you'll bump into a genius and he'll make you rich.

—Ahmet Ertegun

Life is not fair; get used to it.

—Bill Gates

Success in life depends on who your parents were and what circumstances you grew up in.

—Ernest Gallo

Winning is the most important thing in my life, after breathing. Breathing first, winning next.

—George Steinbrenner

We are like the mechanism of a watch: each part is essential.

—Nathan Meyer Rothschild

I figured I wasn't as smart as some of the other fellows, so I had to work twice as hard.

—Joyce Hall

I am convinced that material things can contribute a lot to making one's life pleasant, but, basically, if you do not have very good friends and relatives who matter to you, life will be really empty and sad and material things cease to be important.

—David Rockefeller

Whenever I see an opportunity and a chance to change something, I go at it and I lay out all the facts to everybody . . . And when I come to this space, I'm going to come with talent, I'm going to come with focus. And I'm going to do the job as competitively as the next guy.

—Robert Johnson

My suggestion is to go to school. It will teach you the framework. It teaches you the game.

—Peter van Stolk

If you've got time to lean, you've got time to clean.

—Colonel Harlan Sanders

We all are learning, modifying, or destroying ideas all the time. Rapid destruction of your ideas when the time is right is one of the most valuable qualities you can acquire. You must force yourself to consider arguments on the other side.

—Charles Munger

The hardest lesson I've learned has been to not repeat the dumb mistakes I've made over the years, which are too numerous to list.

—Gerald W. Schwartz

Today more than ever we need creative minds to address the issues of the age. And one of the most urgent is this: How can humanity know so much, achieve so much, and still fail so many people so badly?

—King Abdullah II

I wanted to be the exception to the other kids, but in the right way. We have a lot of suffering in our part of the world, but that suffering is, in a way, a blessing. Obviously, I could not afford to go to school without a scholarship, so that meant I had to excel in order to get one.

—Talal Abu-Ghazaleh

I want to see good financial returns, but also to me there's the extra psychic return of having my creativity and technological vision bear fruit and change the world in a positive way.

—Jeff Bezos

I see what keeps people young: work!

—Ted Turner

If you have competence, you pretty much know its boundaries already. To ask the question (of whether you are past the boundary) is to answer it.

—Charles Munger

I've been in a hurry all my life. I've been in a hurry to succeed, and in a hurry to prove myself.

—Henry Kravis

You talk about capitalism and communism and all that sort of thing, but the important thing is the struggle everybody is engaged in to get better living conditions, and they are not interested too much in the form of government.

—Bernard Baruch

My best and worst boss was the same man—my father. He never—and I mean never—took "I can't" for an answer. He taught me the value system that, to this day, I have continued to practice.

—George Steinbrenner

Wall Street is in the business of making money between now and next Tuesday. We're in the business of building an organization, an institution that we hope will be here 50 years from now. And paying good wages and keeping your people working with you is very good business.

—Jim Sinegal

There is very little knowledge that can't be obtained through effort. With knowledge you can determine the state of any business or opportunity and find a course to gain an advantage.

—Mark Cuban

A merchant who approaches business with the idea of serving the public well has nothing to fear from the competition.

—James Cash Penny

One is only happy in proportion as he makes others feel happy and only useful as he contributes his influences for the finer callings in life.

—Milton Hershey

Commerce is the key driver toward societal change. If everyone that produces the goods the world consumes starts concerning themselves with sustainable, low-impact practices, the world will change.

—Dov Charney

The best minds are not in government. If any were, business would hire them away.

—Ronald Reagan

I'll invest my money in people.

—W. K. Kellogg

[Our] vision for social networks is participatory, visual, based on dialogue. They can be as edgy as they want or as square as they want—it's up to them.

—Tom Anderson and Chris De Wolfe

I believe that the profits will come from the quality of your creative products. Since the beginning, I've always wanted to develop a self-feeding circle of creative productions: The positive financial returns from one show would be used to develop and create a new show, and so on.

—Guy Laliberte

Smart is an elusive concept. There's a certain sharpness, an ability to absorb new facts. To ask an insightful question. To relate to domains that may not seem connected at first. A certain creativity that allows people to be effective.

—Bill Gates

Just about the time you teach a horse to eat hay, the horse dies.

—Jim Sinegal

No sir; the first thing is character, because a man I do not trust could not get money from me on all the bonds in Christendom.

—J. P. Morgan, when asked by a Congressional investigating committee in 1912 whether bankers issued commercial credit only to people who already had money or property

Better to ask twice than lose your way once.

—Sir James Dyson

I've never been surprised about what happened to me. I've put in hard work to get to this point. It's like when you become a lawyer—if you're bustin' your ass, you're not surprised when you get your degree. I came in to win, you know. This is why I stay up late while other people are sleeping; this is why I don't go out to the Hamptons.

—Sean "P. Diddy" Combs

For instance, if you were in a burning building with a hundred people and there was only one door to the outside, do you think your survival rate would be better if that same building had multiple doors leading out? Of course it would. Life and business are no different in the planning stages. Always assume there will be a fire.

—Todd McFarlane

It's the way I work. I sleep 12 hours and then work 24 hours. I've worked those irregular hours for the past three years. It's better to stay up day and night to come up with ideas. I usually get inspiration for game designing by working this schedule.

—Satoshi Tajiri

If you're going to enjoy the picnic that life really is, you'd better learn to like yourself not despite your flaws and so-called deficits, but because of them.

—Paul Orfalea

The feeling of accomplishment is more real and satisfying than finishing a good meal—or looking at one's accumulated wealth.

—Jim Henson

I urge one and all to live this life as if there is no reward in the afterlife, and do it in a moral way that makes it better for you and for those around you and leaves this world a little better place than when you found it.

—Hugh Hefner

If people want to change, they will. If they don't want to, it's hard to make them do so. The current interest in the environment is a good thing. The best way to make a contribution in fashion is to promote the idea that a fundamental interest in preserving the environment is itself fashionable.

—Giorgio Armani

While I am proud of a number of accomplishments, there are real costs to being unreasonable. Long hours. Too little time with family. A near incapacity for, as they say, stopping and smelling the roses.

—Eli Broad

What matters is where you want to go. Focus in the right direction!

—Donald Trump

If the cart is politics and the horse is the economy, then we have to put the horse before the cart and not the other way around.

—Mohammad bin Rashid Al Maktoum

If I had learned education I would not have had time to learn anything else.

—Cornelius Vanderbilt

If you learn late, you pass it on to people so they can learn early. It's a step process.

—Russell Simmons

I don't like to see this type of activity. Eventually, if this bubble bursts, I think that people will be left holding the bag. I don't want to be around when that happens.

—Bernard Madoff

Celebrate your successes. Find some humor in your failures. Don't take yourself so seriously. Loosen up, and everybody around you will loosen up. Have fun. Show enthusiasm—always.

—Sam Walton

Top 25 Billionaires of 2009

Forbes magazine's 2009 list of the top 25 billionaires (weath in billions of dollars in parentheses). All are United States citizens unless otherwise indicated.

1. William Gates III ($40)
2. Warren Buffett ($37)
3. Carlos Slim Helu – Mexico ($35)
4. Lawrence Ellison ($22.5)
5. Ingvar Kamprad – Sweden/Switzerland ($22)
6. Karl Albrecht – Germany ($21.5)
7. Mukesh Ambani – India ($19.5)
8. Lakshmi Mittal – India ($19.3)
9. Theo Albrecht – Germany (18.8)
10. Amancio Ortega – Spain ($18.3)
11. Jim Walton ($17.8)
12. Alice Walton ($17.6)
12. Christy Walton ($17.6)
12. S. Robson Walton ($17.6)
15. Bernard Arnault – France ($16.5)
16. Li Ka-shing – Hong Kong ($16.2)
17. Michael Bloomberg ($16.0)
18. Stefan Persson – Sweden ($14.5)
19. Charles Koch ($14)
19. David Koch ($14)
21. Liliane Bettencourt – France ($13.4)
22. Prince Alwaleed Bin Talal Alsaud – Saudi Arabia ($13.3)
23. Michael Otto – Germany ($13.2)
24. David Thomson – Canada ($13)
25. Michael Dell ($12.3)

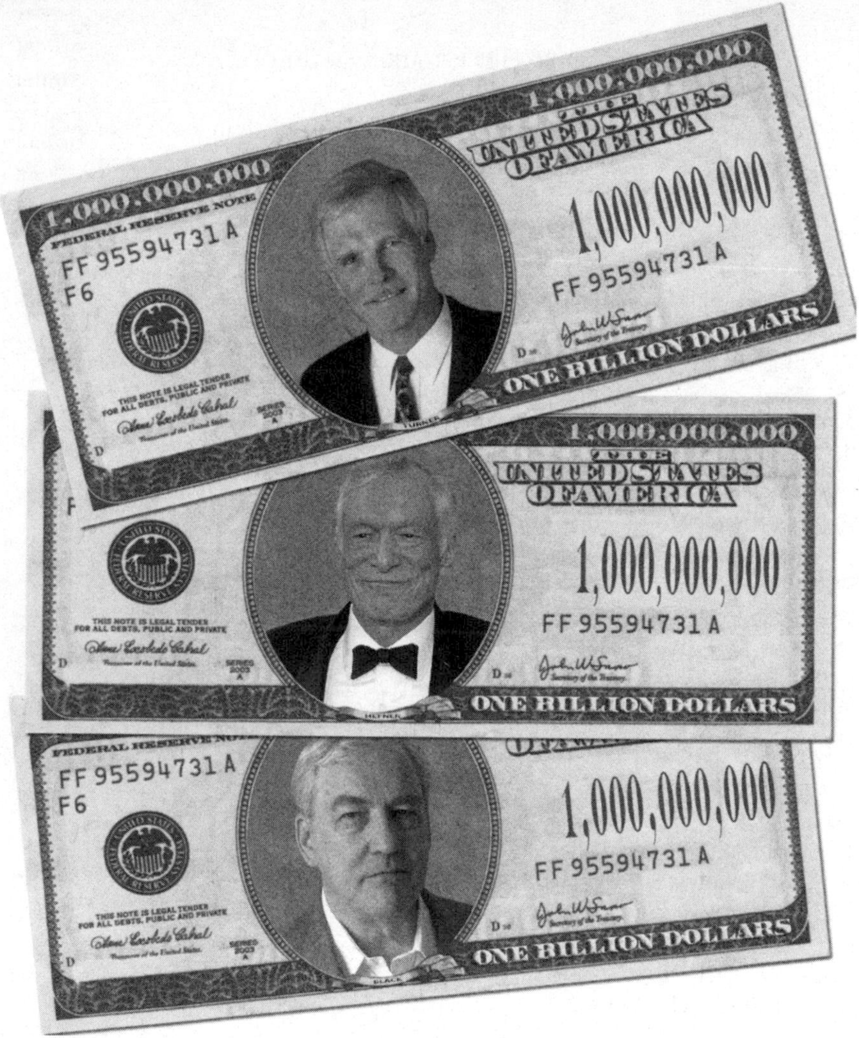

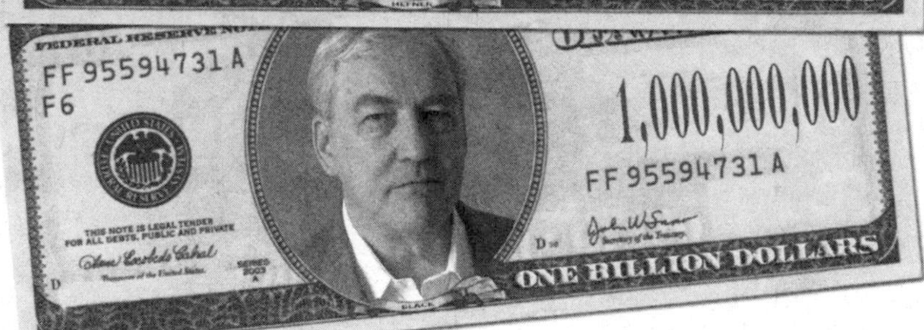

1,000,000,000
FEDERAL RESERVE NOTE
THE UNITED STATES OF AMERICA
FF 95594731 A
F6
1,000,000,000
FF 95594731 A
THIS NOTE IS LEGAL TENDER FOR ALL DEBTS, PUBLIC AND PRIVATE
ONE BILLION DOLLARS
1,000,000,000
THE UNITED STATES OF AMERICA
1,000,000,000
FF 95594731 A
THIS NOTE IS LEGAL TENDER FOR ALL DEBTS, PUBLIC AND PRIVATE
ONE BILLION DOLLARS
FEDERAL RESERVE NOTE
FF 95594731 A
F6
1,000,000,000
FF 95594731 A
THIS NOTE IS LEGAL TENDER FOR ALL DEBTS, PUBLIC AND PRIVATE
ONE BILLION DOLLARS

Selected Quoted Sources

Abramovich, Roman, Russian petroleum investor and sportsman

Abu-Ghazaleh, Talal, Chairman and founder of the Talal Abu-Ghazaleh Organization (intellectual property protection and accounting)

Adulyadej, Bhumibol, King of Thailand, (reputed to be worth $35 billion)

Aigner, Julie, Founder of Baby Einstein videos for children

Al Maktoum bin Rashid, Sheik Mohammad, Prime minister and vice president of the United Arab Emirates, and ruler of Dubai

Albrecht, Karl, German co-founder of Aldi discount supermarket chain and reputed to be the richest person in Germany

Alda, Alan, American film and stage actor

Aleichem, Sholom, Pen name of Sholem Naumovich Rabinovich, Russian author of Yiddish literature

Alexander, Scott, American author

Al-Fayed, Mohamed, Egyptian-British businessman, owner of Harrod's department store

Alwaleed Bin Talal Alsaud, Prince, member of the Saudi Royal family, and entrepreneur and international investor

Allen, Woody, American film director, writer, actor, comedian, musician, and playwright

Ambani, Mukesh, Indian businessman, chairman of Reliance Industries

Amis, Martin, Contemporary English novelist

Amos, Wally, Founder of Famous Amos Cookies

Anderson, John, President of Topa Equities

Anderson, Tom, Co-creator of MySpace

Annenberg, Walter, American publisher, philanthropist, and diplomat

Armani, Giorgio, Italian clothing designer

Arnault, Bernard, Chairman of Moët Hennesy Louis Vuiton

Ash, Mary Kay, Founder of the Mary Kay cosmetics line

Ash, Roy, Co-founder of Litton Industries

Astor, John, Jacob, American fur trading and real estate businessman, the first multi-millionaire in the United States (his fortune at his death was more than $100 billion in present-day dollars)

Astor, Nancy, First woman to serve in the British House of Commons

Austen, Jane, 18th-century English novelist

Bacon, Sir Francis, 17th-century English philospher, statesman, jurist, and author

Baldwin, Billy, Society decorator

Ballmer, Steve, CEO of Microsoft

Balzac, Honoré de, 19th-century French novelist and playwright

Banks, Ernie, Chicago Cubs baseball player

Baraka, Amiri, African-American poet, playwright, activist

Barnum, Phineas, T., Founder of the Ringling Bros. and Barnum & Bailey Circus

Barr, Amelia, 19th-century British-American novelist

Baruch, Bernard, 20th-century American financier and presidential advisor

Bean, Leon, Leonwood, Founder of L. L. Bean

Beatles, The, British rock band

Beaverbrook, Max Aitken, Lord, 20th-century Canadian newspaper magnate

Belloc, Hilaire, 20th-century French writer and historian

Beng, Kwek, Leng, Singapore venture capital investor

Berlusconi, Silvio, Media mogul and Prime Minister of Italy

Bevan, Aneurin, 20th-century British politician

Bezos, Jeff, Founder and CEO of Amazon.com

Billings, Josh, 19th-century American humorist

Black, Conrad, Canadian newspaper publisher

Blank, Arthur, Founder of Home Depot

Blixseth, Tim, Founder of Yellowstone Club resorts and golf courses

Bloomberg, Michael, American businessman and philanthropist, Mayor of New York City

Boesky, Ivan, American investor, notorious for his role in the "Wall Street insider trading scandal"

Bond, Alan, Australian businessman and sportsman
Bosch, Robert, German founder of automotive components company
Bourdet, Edouard, 20th-century French playwright
Branson, Richard, British founder of Virgin Records and Virgin Airlines
Brin, Sergey, American founder of Google, Inc.
Broad, Eli, American financier, art collector, and philanthropist
Bronfman, Sr., Edgar, Canadian businessman and philanthropist
Brooks, David, American political and cultural journalist and commentator
Bryan, William, Jennings, 20th-century American politician
Buffett, Warren, American investor, chairman of Berkshire-Hathaway, and #1 on the 2008 *Forbes* list of world's wealthiest people
Burns, Charles, Montgomery "Monty," TV cartoon character, Homer Simpon's tightfisted boss
Burton, Sir Richard, 19th-century English explorer and writer
Bushnell, Nolan, founder of Atari and Chuck E. Cheese's
Butler, Samuel, 19th-century British novelist
Butler, Geezer, English musician, bass player of Black Sabbath rock band
Byron, George Gordon, Lord, 19th-century British poet
Canfield, Jack, American motivational speaker and co-creater of the "Chicken Soup for the Soul" series
Caplan, Mitchell, CEO of E*Trade Group, Inc.
Cardenas, Robert, retired U.S. Air Force general and business executive
Carnegie, Andrew, 19th-century Scots-American steel industrialist and philanthropist
Case, Steve, CEO of America Online
Chanel, Coco, French fashion designer
Charles V, Holy Roman Emperor and King of Spain
Charney, Dov, Founder of American Apparel
Chekhov, Anton, 19th-century Russian author and playwright
Chesterton, G. K., 20th-century English author and mystery novelist
Christie, Agatha, 20th-century English crime writer

Chrysler, Walter, Founder of the Chrysler automobile empire
Clason, George, Soldier, businessman, and writer
Clitheroe, Paul, Australian financier and author, founder of ipac Securities
Clough, Arthur, Hugh, 19th-century British poet
Cocks, Sir Barnett, 20th-century British politician
Cohen, Ben, Co-founder of Ben & Jerry's ice cream company
Combs, Sean, "P. Diddy," American rap music producer and entrepreneur
Conwell, Russell Herman, 19th-century minister and educator, founder of Temple University
Cooley, Mason, American writer and aphorist
Cork, Kenneth, British lawyer
Craig, Jenny, Founder of Jenny Craig, Inc. weight-loss program
Csikszentmihalyi, Mihaly, 20th-century Hungarian psychologist
Cuban, Mark, Founder of MicroSolutions and Landmark Theaters
Dali, Salvador, 20th-century Spanish surrealist artist
Davis, Bette, 20th-century American film actress
Davis, Marvin, American petroleum industrialist, investor, and philanthropist
de Vries, Peter, 20th-century American editor and novelist
De Wolfe, Chris, Co-creator of MySpace social networking website
Dell, Michael, American businessman, founder of Dell, Inc. computers
DeLuca, Fred, Founder of Subway sandwich chain
Dennis, Felix, British magazine publisher
DeVos, Richard, M., Founder of Amway
Dickens, Charles, 19th-century British novelist
Didion, Joan, 20th-century American journalist and author
Diller, Barry, Television executive, creator of Fox Brodcasting and USA Broadcasting
Dirkson, Everett, 20th-century American politician
Disney, Walt, Film producer, founder of Walt Disney Company
Disney, Roy, Senior executive of the Walt Disney Company
Drucker, Peter, Ameican author and management consultant
Dylan, Bob, American pop and folk musician

Dyson, James, Sir, British industrial designer, inventor of the Dual Cyclone bagless vacuum cleaner
Eastman, George, 20th-century American inventor, founder of the Eastman Kodak film company
Edison, Thomas, 19th-century American inventor and businessman
Eikerenkootter, Frederick, "Reverend Ike," 20th-century American televangelist
Eisner, Michael, Former CEO of the Walt Disney Company
Elizabeth II, Current British monarch
Ellison, Larry, Co-founder and CEO of the Oracle Corporation
Emerson, Ralph, Waldo, 19th-century American essayist and poet
Epictetus, 1st-century B.C. Greek Stoic philosopher
Erdman, Paul, American economist
Ertegun, Ahmet, Turkish-American record producer, co-founder of Atlantic Records
Fielding, Henry, British novelist
Fields, W. C., American film and stage actor
Fields, Debbi, CEO of Mrs. Fields Cookies
Firestone, Harvey, S., Founder of the Firestone Tire and Rubber Company
Fitzgerald, F., Scott, 20th-century American novelist
Forbes, Bertie Charles, Scots-American founder of *Forbes* magazine and publishing empire
Forbes, Malcolm, S., Former publisher of *Forbes* magazine
Ford, Henry, Founder of the Ford Motor Company
Ford, Edsel, Son of Henry Ford, president of Ford Motor Company 1919–1943
Franklin, Benjamin, Founding Father of the U.S., author, scientist, statesman
Friedland, Robert, Chairman and director of Ivanhoe Energy and Ivanhoe Mines
Galbraith, John, Kenneth, Canadian-American economist
Gallo, Ernest, Co-founder of E. & J. Gallo Winery
Gandhi, Mohandas, K., 20th-century political and spiritual leader of India
Gates, William "Bill," II, Founder of Microsoft
Geffen, David, Music, film, and theatrical producer
Geller, Uri, Author and psychic

Geneen, Harold, S., American businessman, former president of the ITT Corporation

Gerstner, Louis V., American businessman, former chairman of IBM

Getty, J., Paul, American industrialist, founder of Getty Oil

Getty, Gordon, Composer and son of J. Paul Getty

Giannini, A. P., Founder of Bank of America

Gillette, King, Inventor of the safety razor and founder of the company that bears his name

Goizueta, Roberto, Chairman, director, and CEO of the Coca-Cola Company, 1980–1997

Goldsmith, Oliver, 18th-century British poet and novelist

Googe, Barnabe, 16th-century English poet

Gotti, John, 20th-century Mafia crime boss

Gould, Jay, 19th-century financier and railroad developer

Graham, Katharine, 20th-century American newspaper publisher

Graves, Robert, 20th-century British poet and essayist

Gray, Thomas, 18th-century English poet and professor

Greely, Horace, 19th-century newspaper editor, founder of the Liberal Republican Party

Green, Sir Philip, British retail stores magnate

Greenberg, Maurice, American insurance and investment executive, former CEO of A.I.G insurance empire

Greenspan, Alan, American economist and former chairman of the Federal Reserve

Hall, Joyce, Founder of Hallmark Greeting Cards

Hammer, Armand, American businessman and philanthropist

Harriman, Edward, H., 19th-century railroad developer, president of the Union Pacific and South Pacific lines

Hayes, James, L., Educator and American Management Association president

Hearst, William, Randolph, 19th–20th century American newspaper publisher

Hefner, Christie, Former chairman and CEO of Playboy Enterprises

Hefner, Hugh, Founder of Playboy Enterprises

Heinlein, Robert, A., 20th-century American science fiction author

Heinz, Henry J., German-American businessman, founder of the Heinz foodstuffs corporation

Henson, Jim, Founder of Henson Associates and creator of the Muppets

Hepburn, Katharine, 20th-century American stage and film actress

Hershey, Milton, Founder of the Hershey chocolate empire

Hill, Napoleon, American author of *Think and Grow Rich*

Hilton, Conrad, Founder of Hilton Hotel chain

Holmes, Oliver Wendell, Sr., 19th-century American author and physician

Hook, Harold, American businessman, CEO of American General Corp.

Horace, 1st-century B.C. Roman lyric poet

Howe, Edgar, Watson, American novelist and newspaper and magazine editor

Hughes, Howard, American industrialist, aviator, and motion picture director and producer

Huizenga, Wayne, Founder of Blockbuster Video, Waste Management, Inc., and AutoNation

Hunt, H. L., American petroleum entrepreneur

Hunt, Nelson, Bunker, Oil company executive

Hunt, Ray, Lee, Chairman of Hunt Oil company

Hurst, Fannie, 20th-century American novelist

Icahn, Carl, American financier and private equity investor

Immelt, Jeffrey, American businessman, chairman of General Electric

Iococca, Lee, American businessman, former president and CEO of the Chrysler Corporation

Jacobs, Irwin, L., Chairman of Genmar boat builders

Jamail, Joseph, D., American attorney specializing in personal injury suits

James, Henry, 19th-century American author

Jobs, Steve, American businessman, co-founder, chairman, and CEO of Apple Inc.

Johnson, Robert, Co-founder of the Black Entertainment Television network

Johnson, Samuel, 18th-century English author, poet, and critic

Johnson, Ervin, "Magic," Basketball star and franchise entrepreneur

Johnson, Sheila, C., Co-founder of Black Entertainment Television

Johnson, John, Founder of Johnson Publishing Company and publisher of *Ebony* magazine

Jonson, Ben, 17th-century English playwright

Ka-shing, Li, Hong Kong plastics industry mogul

Kaiser, Henry, J., American shipbuilder and automobile executive

Kamprad, Ingvar, Swedish founder of Ikea Home Furnishings chain

Kelleher, Herb, Founder of Southwest Airlines

Kellogg, W. K., Founder of the breakfast cereal empire

Kerkorian, Kirk, American investor with interests in real estate and the entertainment and automobile industries

Khodorkovsky, Mikhail, Russian petroleum investor, Russia's wealthiest person before being imprisoned for fraud

Kiam, Victor, American entrepreneur, former owner of Remington Products and the New England Patriots football team

Kiyosaki, Robert, American investor, businessman, and author of *Rich Dad, Poor Dad*

Kluge, John, Media mogul, whose holdings indlude Metromedia

Knight, Philip, Founder of Nike

Kravis, Henry, American financier and investor, co-founder of Kohlberg Kravis Roberts & Co. private equity firm

Kroc, Ray, Founder of the McDonald's fast-food empire

Laliberte, Guy, French impresario, creator of the Cirque du Soleil

Lauder, Ronald, American businessman, diplomat, and art collector

Lauder, Estee, Co-founder of Estee Lauder Companies, Inc.

LeBoeuf, Michael, American business author

Lewis, Peter, CEO of Progressive Insurance Company

Lewis, Joseph, British investor, head of the Tavistock Group holding company

Lipper, Michael, A. Founder of Lipper, Inc., financial information service

Lucas, George, Founder of Lucasfilms

Luce, Henry, R., Founder of Time, Inc. publishing empire

Marlowe, Christopher, 16th-century English poet
Marriott, J. Willard, Founder of the Marriott hotel chain
Marx, Karl, 19th-century Russian political economist
Maugham, W., Somerset, 20th-century British playwright and novelist
McFarlane, Todd, Comic books and toy entrepreneur, creator of Spawn fantasy series
McGovern, William, Founder of MCI communications corporation
McLuhan, Marshall, Canadian educator, philosopher, and scholar
McNealy, Scott, CEO of Sun Microsystems
Mellon, Andrew, 20th-century banker, industrialist, philanthropist, Secretary of the Treasury
Melville, Herman, 19th-century American novelist
Millman, Dan, Author and motivational speaker
Mittal, Lakshmi, Indian industrialist, reputed to be India's wealthiest person
Monaghan, Tom, Founder of Domino's Pizza
Moore, Michael, American filmmaker
Moore, Gordon, Co-founder of Intel Computer chip empire
Morgan, J. P., 19th-century American financier whose wealth made him the country's most influential business figure
Morita, Akio, Japanese businessman, founder of Sony
Munger, Charles, Vice-chairman of Berkshire Hathaway
Murdoch, Rupert, Australian media mogul, chairman of the News Corporation
Musk, Elon, Founder of PayPal and SpaceX
Newmark, Craig, Founder of Craigslist internet social and commercial network
Obama, Barack, The 44th and current president of the United States
Ogilvy, David, Founder of Ogilvy & Mather advertising agency
Omidyar, Pierre, Founder of eBay internet sales network
Onassis, Aristotle, 20th-century Greek shipping magnate
O'Reilly, Bill, Political commentator
Orfalea, Paul, CEO of Kinko's
Orman, Suze, Financial commentator and TV personality

Packard, Vance, 20th-century American journalist and author of *The Status Seekers*

Page, Larry, Co-founder of Google

Pahlavi, Farah, Widow of the former Shah of Iran

Parker, Dorothy, 20th-century American writer

Patterson, John, Henry, Founder of National Cash Register

Penny, James, Cash, Co-founder of JC Penney

Philip, Prince, Duke of Edinburgh, husband of Queen Elizabeth II

Picasso, Pablo, 20th-century Spanish painter

Pickens, T., Boone, American petroleum investor, chairman of BP Capital Management

Plutarch, 1st-century Roman historian and biographer

Pope, Alexander, 18th-century English poet and essayist

Popeil, Ron, American televsision infomercial star

Prada, Miuccia, Italian founder of Prada fashion empire

Pritchard, Michael, Bassist of punk rock band Green Day

Quant, Mary, British clothing designer

Racine, Jean, 17th-century French playwright

Rancic, Bill, One of the winners on Donald Trump's "The Apprentice" television show

Ray, Rachel, American food and lifestyle television star

Reagan, Ronald, 40th president of the United States, governor of California, actor

Redstone, Sumner, American telecommunications magnate, head of National Amusements (includes CBS, Viacom, MTV)

Reinhardt, Gottfried, German film director and producer

Revson, Charles, Chairman of Revlon Cosmetics

Rockefeller, John, D., 19th-century American petroleum entrepreneur and philanthropist

Rockefeller, Winthrop, Governor of Arkansas and philanthropist

Rockefeller, David, Former chairman of Chase Manhattan Bank and philanthropist

Roddick, Anita, Founder of The Body Shop Cosmetics chain

Rogers, Will, 20th-century Ameican comedian and actor

Rohn, Jim, American motivational speaker

Rose, Billy, 20th-century American theatrical impresario

Rothschild, Mayer, Amschel, 18th-century German founder of the House of Rothschild banking empire

Rothschild, Nathan, Meyer, 19th-century British financier involved in the international Rothschild family banking emire

Rowling, J. K., British author of the Harry Potter series

Runyon, Damon, 20th-century American author

Sabinci, Sakip, Turkish entrepreneur and investor

Salter, Mary, Jo, 20th-century American poet

Sanders, Colonel, Harland, Founder of Kentucky Fried Chicken

Sarnoff, Robert, W., former chairman of RCA Corporation

Schmidt, Eric, Chairman and CEO of Google Inc.

Schopenhauer, Arthur, 19th-century German philosopher

Schrempp, Jurgen, German businessman, former CEO of DaimlerChrysler

Schultz, Howard, Founder of Starbucks coffee shop chain

Schulze, Richard, Founder of Best Buy appliance chain

Schwab, Charles, Founder of the world's largest discount brokerage house

Schwartz, Gerald, W., Canadian co-founder of CanWest Global Communications Inc, and Onex Corporation

Sculley, John, Former president of Pepsico, then CEO of Apple

Shakespeare, William, 17th-century English poet and playwright

Sharp, Issy, Founder of the Four Seasons hotel chain

Shaw, George, Bernard, 20th-century Irish playwright and critic

Simmons, Russell, American hip-hop music producer

Simon, Norton, American industrial and investor and art patron

Sinegal, Jim, Founder of Costco

Sloan, P., Alfred, former head of General Motors

Smith, Frederick, W., Founder of Federal Express (FedEx)

Soros, George, American investor, founder of Soros Fund Management and philanthropist

Spielberg, Steven, American film director and producer

Stamp, Sir Josiah, 19th-century director of the Bank of England

Stein, Gertrude, 20th-century American writer
Steinbrenner, George, American shipping executive and owner of the New York Yankees
Stevens, Wallace, 20th-century American poet
Stewart, Martha, American TV host, author, and magazine publisher of home decorating and entertaining publications
Stout, Rex, 20th-century American crime writer
Sukhorukov, Leonid, S., Ukrainian author and commentator
Swid, Stephen, Chairman and CEO of SESAC
Syrus, Publius, 1st-century B.C. Roman writer of maxims
Tajiri, Satoshi, Japanese video game designer, inventor of Pokemon
Taubman, Alfred, A., Former chairman of Sotheby's auction gallery
Taylor, Jack, C., Founder of Enterprise Rent-A-Car
Theognis, 6th-century B.C. Greek poet
Theresa, Mother, Albanian nun who founded the Missionaries of Charity in Kolkata, India
Thomas, Dave, Founder of Wendy's fast-food chain
Todd, Mike, 20th-century American theater and film producer
Trollope, Anthony, 19th-century British novelist
Trump, Donald, American real estate developer, TV personality and author
Trump, Ivanka, American businesswoman, fashion model, daughter of Donald Trump
Turner, Ted, American media entrepreneur and sportsman
Twain, Mark, 19th-century American novelist
Updike, John, 20th-century American novelist
van Stolk, Peter, Founder and CEO of Jones Soda
Vanderbilt, Cornelius, "Commodore," 19th-century American railroad and shipping magnate
Voltaire, François-Marie, 18th-century French essayist and playwright
von Mises, Ludwig, 20th-century Austrian economist
Waitt, Theodore, Co-founder of Gateway computers
Walker, Madam, C.J., 19th-century American manufacturer of hair products for African-American women, reputedly the first female to become a millionaire solely through her own efforts

Walton, Sam, American businessman, founder of Wal-Mart and Sam's Club
Wang, Vera, American fashion designer
Ward, Artemus, 19th-century American humorist
Warner, Jack, L., 20th-century American motion picture producer
Watson, Thomas, Founder of International Business Machines (IBM)
Weil, Sanford, I., Former chairman of Citicorp
Welch, John, Former chairman of General Electric
Wharton, Edith, 19th-century American novelist
Whitehorn, Katherine, 20th-century British journalist and writer
Whitney, John, Hay, Publisher of the New York *Herald Tribune*, U.S. Ambassador to the UK
Willians, Tennessee, 20th-century American playwright
Winfrey, Oprah, TV personality, host, and entrepreneur
Wonder, Stevie, American pop musician
Woolworth, F. W., Founder of Woolworth's "5 & 10" chain of stores
Wynn, Steve, American casino resort developer
Yunus, Muhammad, Bangladesh banker and originator of micro-credit
Ziglar, Zig, Motivational speaker